Public Access to Information for Development

DIRECTIONS IN DEVELOPMENT
Public Sector Governance

Public Access to Information for Development

A Guide to the Effective Implementation of Right to Information Laws

Victoria L. Lemieux and Stephanie E. Trapnell

WORLD BANK GROUP

Contents

Boxes

Figures

Maps

Tables

Foreword

"Openness," "accountability," and "transparency" seem to be on everyone's lips today. Thanks to national democratization movements, the Open Government Partnership with 69 member countries, international organizations such as the United Nations and the World Bank, and the leadership and encouragement of civil society organizations, we hear loudly and clearly that transparency is a key to holding governments accountable. Further, we understand that transparency depends on the critical element of access: the right of a country's people to access information created and maintained by their government and governmental institutions. Having a freedom of information law—increasingly referred to as a right to information (RTI) law—on the books is a first big step to fight corruption and shed light on government activities. Yet making the law work every day is a far greater challenge, one that is faced by every country with such a law in place. For example, the Freedom of Information Act in the United States is nearly 50 years old and is still evolving, with significant revisions nearly every decade. Those changes attempt to deal with real-life experiences with the law, but efforts to enact or update any RTI law illustrate the perils of defining outcomes and measuring a law's effectiveness, much less making improvements amid political considerations.

How will you let citizens know about the law and what it can do for them? What is an openness culture, and how do you build one? Can you recruit and train a professional workforce and provide executive support for it? Where do you find models for developing procedures and practices to receive and track requests, to gather potentially responsive records, to process documents in various formats for release, and to anticipate demand and proactively disclose records? What must one do to create an infrastructure for managing and preserving records? It is simple but true: If you do not have the records to begin with, the right to access is hollow. Are you able to ensure the integrity of the records and maintain them in formats so that people can not only see what their government is doing but also document their rights? Is it possible to ensure that oversight authorities have a sound basis for suggesting corrective actions and best practices, and that anyone, including information intermediaries, can transform the information for a variety of uses?

This guide's insights into effective implementation and the complementary case studies will be welcomed by those charged with daily responsibility for managing government records and responding to requests for them. Equally, researchers and advocates for openness will find the guide compelling reading for its history of RTI and discussion of effectiveness indicators and special topics, such as balancing privacy and secrecy. I congratulate the authors for setting out a cogent framework for a complex subject and providing valuable resources for those of us who care deeply about making access to information a meaningful right.

Miriam Nisbet
Former Director of the Office of Government
Information Services (OGIS)
United States

Preface

With more than 100 right to information (RTI) laws—also called freedom of information or access to information laws—now in place globally, the groundwork has been laid to advance more transparent, accountable, and inclusive governance as a pathway to poverty reduction and economic development. In this guide, we explore the historical development of RTI laws, the factors that drive passage and effective implementation of these laws, the operation of the laws, and the impact of these laws in different country contexts and sectors, as well as the challenges of measuring the contribution of RTI laws to development outcomes.

The guide is based on two years of research studying how RTI has been implemented in countries in different regions and with varying income levels around the world. These experiences have been captured in the companion volume to this guide, *Right to Information: Case Studies on Implementation.*[1] Our research over this period has aimed to develop a theoretical framework by which to identify the drivers of effective implementation of RTI laws, which we discuss in chapter 2 of this guide, as well as to support measurement of effective implementation. Measuring effective implementation of RTI laws is a challenging undertaking, as we discuss in chapter 4—what does it mean to have effectively implemented an RTI law? What aspects of a law have to be operational before it can be said to have been effectively implemented? Which factors are most critical to the effective implementation of RTI laws? And why does effective implementation of RTI matter? These are all questions that we address in this guide.

In writing the guide, we were motivated by the desire to help policy makers, public officials, and development specialists better understand how to ensure that RTI laws not only exist but actively function to achieve development outcomes. Our intended audience includes development practitioners, civil society organizations, and public officials responsible for RTI administration. We have oriented the guide to policy makers interested in the implementation practices that follow from RTI laws and policies. It is our hope that these readers will benefit from not only the discussion of broad processes of RTI implementation, but also the operational guidance on institutionalization of RTI processes within public agencies. We have also inserted significant discussion of broad themes such as privacy, sequencing, and measurement. We hope these topics will be of interest to students, academics, and professionals working on issues of open government and transparency in such areas as law, procurement, open data, rulemaking, and delivery of services in, for example, health and education. Finally, we hope that academics will find innovative ways to further the research into RTI implementation and possibly extend their inquiries to longer-term outcomes and impacts.

Though not essentially a "how to" manual, the guide discusses what our research has identified as the key drivers of RTI implementation success, the elements that are necessary for effective operation of these laws, and the monitoring and evaluation of their effects. We hope that the guide will serve as a valuable resource for all those working toward adoption and implementation of the right to information.

Victoria L. Lemieux
Stephanie E. Trapnell

Note

1. Stephanie E. Trapnell, ed., *Right to Information: Case Studies on Implementation.* Right to Information Series. Washington, DC: World Bank.

Acknowledgments

The authors would like to acknowledge the financial support of the Nordic Trust Fund, without which this publication would not have been possible. Many people contributed to making this publication much better than it otherwise would have been. We would like to thank, in particular, Jeff Thindwa, who chaired the publication peer review committee, and our formal peer reviewers: Toby Mendel, of the Centre for Law and Democracy, and Hannah George, Laura Agosta, and Marcos Mendiburu of the World Bank. We would also like to thank colleagues who took time to provide informal feedback on the development of the publication: Gilbert Sendugwa of the Africa Freedom of Information Centre and David Satola and Luis Esquivel of the World Bank. Finally, we are grateful to Laryssa Chiu for her outstanding administrative assistance and to the entire publication production team at the World Bank.

About the Authors

Victoria L. Lemieux is a senior public sector specialist (Transparency and Information Management) at the World Bank and an associate professor of archival studies at the University of British Columbia (on leave). She has held positions as a professional archivist, records manager, and risk manager in the public and private sectors, and in higher education as an administrator and educator. She has also consulted for the United Nations, the Commonwealth Secretariat, and the World Bank. Her current research is focused on risk to the availability of trustworthy records, in particular in financial contexts, and how these risks impact transparency, financial stability, public accountability, and human rights. She holds a doctorate from University College London (archival studies, 2002), which focused on the information-related causes of the Jamaican banking crisis; since 2005, she has been a certified information systems security professional (CISSP). She is the recipient of several awards and distinctions for her research and professional contributions, including a 2015 World Bank Big Data Innovation Award and the 2015 Emmett Leahy Award.

Stephanie E. Trapnell is a PhD candidate in sociology at George Mason University and served as a founding team member and research manager for the Public Accountability Mechanisms (PAM) Initiative and the Actionable Governance Indicators (AGI) Initiative, both at the World Bank. She is a specialist in open government, accountability, and measurement and is the author of *User's Guide to Measuring Corruption and Anti-corruption*, published by the United Nations Development Programme (2015). Her current research is focused on networks, implementation processes, and outcomes in right to information systems, including civil society engagement and government administration. She holds an MA in international relations and international economics from the Johns Hopkins University, School of Advanced International Studies, and an AB in linguistics from Bryn Mawr College.

Abbreviations

AFIC	Africa Freedom of Information Centre
ATI	access to information
BELA	Bangladesh Environmental Lawyers Association
BGMEA	Bangladesh Garment Manufacturers and Exporters Association
CSO	civil society organization
DIO	departmental information officer
EEI	Enabling Environment Index (CIVICUS)
FDI	foreign direct investment
FOI	freedom of information
FOIA	Freedom of Information Act
G-8	Group of Eight: leaders from Canada, France, Germany, Italy, Japan, the Russian Federation, the United Kingdom, and the United States
G-20	Group of 20: finance ministers and central bank governors from 19 countries and the European Union
GDP	gross domestic product
GPSA	Global Partnership for Social Accountability
GRPs	good regulatory practices
ICCPR	International Covenant on Civil and Political Rights
ICT	information and communication technology
ISO	International Organization for Standardization
IT	information technology
MSR	management system for records
NGO	nongovernmental organization
OAIS	open archival information system
OAS	Organization of American States

OGP	Open Government Partnership
RIDE	RTI Implementation: Drivers of Effectiveness
RTI	right to information

| US$ | United States dollar |
| U Sh | Uganda shilling |

CHAPTER 1

Introduction to the Guide

Laws giving individuals a legal right to access information held by public bodies, commonly referred to as the right to information (RTI), but also known as freedom of information (FOI) or access to information (ATI) laws, are now in place in more than 100 countries globally (see map B1.1.1 in box 1.1).[1] RTI was formally acknowledged by the United Nations in 2011, as part of Article 19 of the Universal Declaration of Human Rights, but the phenomenon of RTI laws began in earnest at the national level well before that time.[2] The movement to secure rights to information from government sources has its origins in mid-20th-century battles for political and civil rights demanded by national-level actors. Today RTI is a key part of the overall global trend toward more transparent and open government, which includes other elements such as protection of whistleblowers, providing access to data in open formats (open data), and requiring senior officials to make asset declarations.[3]

RTI Laws and Their Provisions

An RTI law aims at improving the efficiency of the government and increasing the transparency of its functioning by

- Regularly and reliably providing government documents to the public
- Educating the public on the significance of transparent government
- Facilitating appropriate and relevant use of information in people's lives (World Bank 2013).

According to the World Bank's Public Accountability Mechanisms Initiative, for an RTI law to be an effective and functioning mechanism for transparency, seven factors are key: scope of coverage of disclosures, procedures for accessing information, exemptions to disclosure requirements, enforcement mechanisms, specified deadlines for release of requested information, sanctions for noncompliance, and proactive disclosure (World Bank 2013).

Box 1.1 Tracking the Global Spread and Quality of RTI Laws

The *Global Right to Information Rating* map (map B1.1.1) provides RTI advocates, reformers, legislators, and others with information about RTI laws by country and a rating of the strengths and weaknesses of the legal framework. Countries shaded the darkest have laws that are rated among the best in the world. Countries with no shading still have no RTI law in place.

Map B1.1.1 Global Right to Information Rating Map

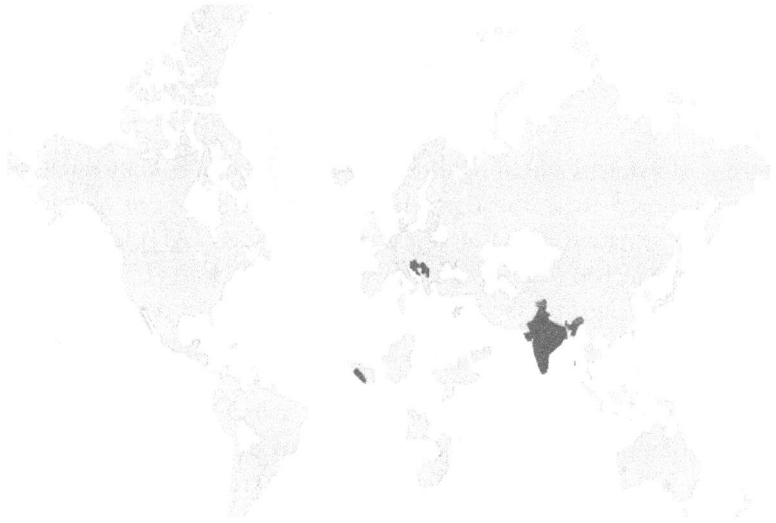

Source: Access Info Europe and the Centre for Law and Democracy.
Note: For current ratings and to explore an interactive map of RTI laws by country go to http://www.rti-rating.org/index.php.

Outcomes of RTI Laws

With the advent of laws specifically establishing RTI, evidence is growing that people around the world have been able to access public information "to expose and prevent corruption, to enhance their ability to participate in public affairs, to protect other human rights, to hold governments to account, to improve service delivery, to facilitate their businesses and to further their own personal goals" (FOIAnet 2013; see also Calland and Bentley 2013).[4]

RTI has been linked to improved accountability, better service delivery, and greater investor confidence. Moreover, people increasingly expect to be able to access information held by public bodies and private entities performing public functions as part of a demand for more transparent, accountable, and inclusive governance. By providing a means for individuals to request information from public authorities, RTI laws reduce the likelihood that public authorities will be able to abuse their control of government information.[5] Access to information also is said to be a key enabler of accountability mechanisms because, by reducing information asymmetry,[6] it provides principals (that is, citizens) with the information they need to hold agents (that is, government officials) to account.[7] Without accountability mechanisms, officials may start to operate in their own interests exclusively, rather than on behalf of the citizens they represent. An example of this would be a "kleptocracy," where corrupt government officials steal public resources, leaving citizens impoverished.

Lack of transparency may also affect service delivery because it can hide corruption and prevent accountability and because members of the public may remain unaware of information about services and how to access them. Inclusive governance means that government operates for the benefit of all members of society, not just a few. Effectively implemented RTI regimes provide marginalized members of society with access to government services and information and the means to demand information in support of their entitlement to legal and human rights, thus helping them to make their voices heard. Effective RTI laws, by institutionalizing rules and procedures for access, also enable other open government mechanisms (for example, open data) to function effectively.[8] Finally, they bind future governments to maintaining RTI.

Progress and Challenges in Implementation

Measuring the level of implementation of RTI laws, and their long-term impact, poses many methodological challenges. A reasonable body of anecdotal evidence exists, along with some systematic empirical research, that demonstrates the value of RTI as a support for transparency, accountability, and inclusive governance. Agreement on the positive impact of RTI is not universal, however. This is, in part, because researchers have not looked much beyond the greater transparency afforded by RTI laws to questions of long-term societal transformation.[9] Some of this evidence is presented in chapter 5.

Regardless of the challenges of measuring impact, it is fair to say that only once RTI laws have been effectively implemented can they truly achieve their full promise. In many countries, unfortunately, overwhelming evidence suggests that effective implementation of the laws continues to present serious challenges and that full realization of the anticipated benefits associated with access to information remains elusive. To be clear, we are not suggesting that effective implementation equates to full implementation of the law. Even partial implementation of an RTI law can lead to positive actions in some contexts. For example, in Pakistan, where a relatively weak law has been implemented, its existence has led to greater transparency through posting of individuals' tax information online. Nevertheless, our focus here is on effective implementation, which emphasizes implementation of those—even partial—elements of an RTI law, in additional to broader societal and governmental conditions, that matter most when the goal is to use the law to increase public access to information and make use of the information gained in service to positive social and economic change.

The following discussion attempts to capture general strengths and weaknesses of RTI systems in the 12 case studies that underpin the research presented

in this guide. It should be considered a general description that highlights prominent characteristics in each system, rather than a comprehensive objective assessment, and it is meant to orient readers who may not be entirely familiar with
each country system presented in the guide. For more detailed information
about the RTI systems in each of the case study countries, readers should refer
to the companion volume to this guide, "Right to Information: Case Studies on
Implementation" (Trapnell 2014).

In reviewing progress on implementation, RTI systems in India, Mexico, the
United Kingdom, and the United States are considered robust but still facing
challenges. India has a vibrant civil society that engages with the RTI system
regularly and at all levels and sectors of implementation, yet it still struggles with
low levels of capacity within the public sector and with many other implementation challenges.[10] Mexico is considered a model RTI system because of its independent and well-funded information commission, which succeeds in enforcing
disclosure obligations on public bodies using a variety of methods, but it has
recently experienced, but overcome, some threats to the robustness of its RTI
regime (Freedominfo.org 2015). The RTI system in the United Kingdom has
succeeded in implementing RTI throughout public bodies by means of its professionalized civil service and the monitoring and enforcement capabilities of an
independent information commission against a backdrop of growing opposition
to RTI from politicians (Cobain 2011).[11] Even though it lacks an information
commission, the United States has been implementing RTI for nearly five
decades, and its RTI system is considered functional, yet characterized by delays
in appeals processing.[12] All this is to say, that even the most effective RTI regimes
face challenges or will experience setbacks at some point.

On the other side of the spectrum are new and struggling RTI systems, where
implementation is either slow in taking hold or has suffered setbacks. Jordan is
still in the early phases of implementing RTI within the public sector, and many
agencies have yet even to develop forms or procedures for requesting access.
Uganda faces general challenges with levels of staff capacity and resources within
the civil service, while the implementation of Moldova's RTI system has not been
supported by any nodal authority or monitoring body (that is, a body that sits
within the executive branch of government and is charged with overseeing
implementation of the RTI law). Public officials in Thailand operate with unclear
policies on the kinds of information that can be released and are subject to severe
sanctions for release of classified information.

In the middle of the spectrum are countries that have implemented RTI with
varying degrees of progress but still face various challenges. Albania's RTI system
is characterized by informal personal networks within the public sector that
substitute for formalized practices, but this makes obtaining information through
RTI procedures problematic for ordinary citizens. Peru and Romania have
engaged civil societies, yet grapple with training, enforcement, and monitoring.
South Africa has an active human rights commission that conducts regular evaluations and training for civil servants but lacks enforcement authority and faces
the challenge of low capacity within the civil service.[13]

Measuring Outcomes to Determine Implementation Effectiveness

All countries face implementation challenges, underscoring the importance of gaining a clearer picture of what drives effective implementation and how it can be achieved and sustained. This guide aims to make a contribution to filling that knowledge gap. A good place to start the discussion is with an explanation of the definition of effective implementation used in this guide. Effectiveness generally means the degree to which something is successful in achieving a desired outcome. The problem of identifying whether the legal RTI has achieved desired outcomes is not trivial.

As outlined above, RTI laws can have many outcomes. At a very basic level, the goal of RTI laws is to allow for the disclosure of information, labeled *first degree* outcomes. At this stage, effectiveness means that RTI rules and procedures, as set forth in RTI laws of generally good initial quality, have been implemented and routinized and support fairness in decision making about disclosure of information, and information is generally disclosed unless there is good reason to withhold it. First-degree outcomes, however, tell us nothing about whether the disclosure of information has led to improved governance or service delivery, or even whether it has supported individual goals. These accountability outcomes, *second degree* outcomes, are more difficult to trace, though we do have evidence. Finally, in the context of development, whether RTI laws contribute to broad socioeconomic change and the goals of poverty reduction or shared prosperity, *third degree* outcomes,[14] is even more difficult to determine, even though these outcomes are often cited as the basis for reform efforts. Figure 1.1 summarizes the different degrees of outcomes in RTI implementation.

Figure 1.1 Projected Degree Outcomes in RTI Implementation

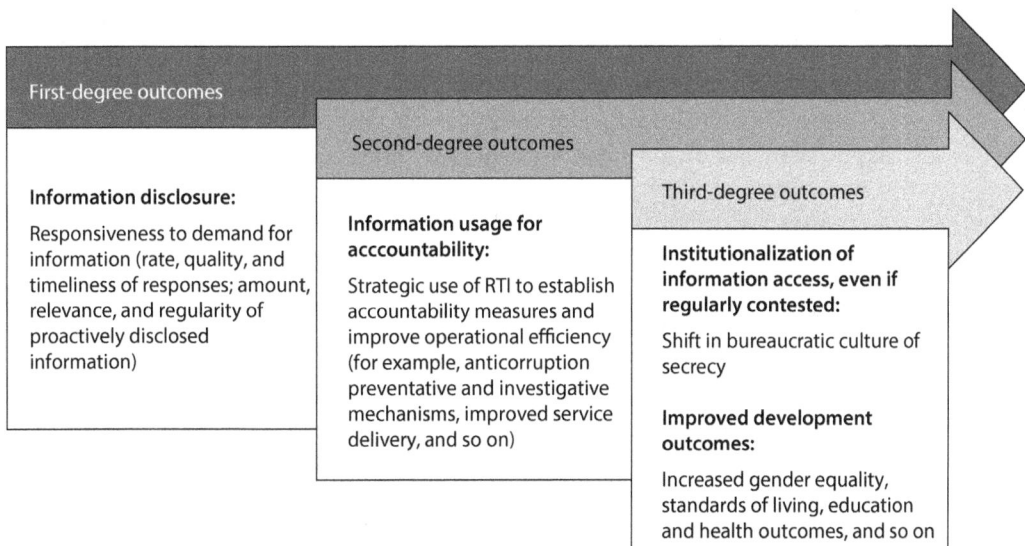

First-degree outcomes

Second-degree outcomes

Third-degree outcomes

Information disclosure:

Responsiveness to demand for information (rate, quality, and timeliness of responses; amount, relevance, and regularity of proactively disclosed information)

Information usage for acccountability:

Strategic use of RTI to establish accountability measures and improve operational efficiency (for example, anticorruption preventative and investigative mechanisms, improved service delivery, and so on)

Institutionalization of information access, even if regularly contested:

Shift in bureaucratic culture of secrecy

Improved development outcomes:

Increased gender equality, standards of living, education and health outcomes, and so on

Source: Trapnell and Lemieux 2014.
Note: RTI = right to information.

From the disclosure of information using an RTI law to development outcomes, the results chain is long and attenuated. For this reason, this guide defines RTI effectiveness as *the capacity of the RTI regime to disclose information as intended by the RTI law in a particular country.* In essence, this is a first degree outcome and the least difficult outcome to measure. It is also the foundation for being able to measure the other outcomes.

That said, it is still not easy to measure even first degree outcomes. There is no quantifiable, reliable measurement of *effective* RTI implementation, defined as first degree outcomes, yet available. Measures of whether a law exists or is of good quality tell us little about how well it has been implemented. Country data on the operation of an RTI law, such as the number of requests, responses, appeals, and proactively disclosed documents, provide a general picture of the volume of requests being processed and information released by administrative systems and may even capture data on timeliness (Worker with Excell 2014). But this type of data offers little information on the quality of responses, relevance of proactively released information to demand, or satisfaction of users. These latter factors are arguably more important to understanding the nature of disclosure than figures on volume and timeliness, because they provide insight into the social and economic impact of RTI laws.

There is also the question of the reliability of the administrative data being published by countries on their performance in RTI systems. This is not necessarily a reflection of intentional obfuscation on the part of governments but, more so, the state of administrative operations within an agency. The absence of, poor quality of, or inconsistent adherence to internal tracking systems for requests, as well as variance in the quality of performance monitoring systems within public bodies, may contribute to imprecise data. Other types of monitoring, such as compliance testing by civil society organizations or oversight bodies on the rate of response, are often feasible only for a sample of agencies, as are external checks on the quality of government responses. Generalizations about the entire set of government agencies with unreliable and inconsistently collected data must be made with qualification. Basing conclusions about effectiveness on administrative data or compliance testing generates a partial understanding of how a system is performing but is far from complete.

In an attempt to encompass a wider frame of understanding about RTI effectiveness than simple data on responsiveness, performance, or the mechanics of implementation, this guide relies upon a framework that focuses on the precursors to implementation effectiveness, that is, what is preventing or facilitating effective implementation in practice. This framework considers the drivers of implementation that lead to good development outcomes, as reflected in so-called success stories in RTI implementation, as well as systems that are struggling with different aspects of implementation. The conclusions in these stories about the drivers of effectiveness in RTI systems are based on a synthesis of the successes and constraints to a functioning RTI system that have been documented in numerous country case studies. Recurring issues, areas of success, and large and small failures have been categorized and grouped so as to generate insight into what matters for RTI effectiveness beyond the parameters of a single case (Trapnell and Lemieux 2014).

Methodology of Underlying Research

The underlying research for this guide employed a thematic synthesis of 12 country case studies that examined the quality and extent of implementation of RTI systems (Trapnell 2014). Its primary aim was to identify drivers of effectiveness for RTI implementation, but consideration of important themes that characterize RTI implementation (for example, innovations, good practices, challenges, and so on) was a secondary goal. Rather than a reorganization and summary of information that characterizes a literature review, thematic synthesis aims to identify the recurring themes or issues in a collection of primary research and to generate an analytical understanding that extends beyond the conclusions of the individual cases.[15]

Sampling of Cases

Purposive sampling was used to select cases, as a form of nonprobability sampling in which decisions about the sample of cases were strategic and tied to the objectives of the study. The aim of purposive sampling is not prediction, but interpretative explanation that extends beyond the analysis of each individual case. Results are not generalizable to an entire population without qualification. Instead, they contribute to a more sophisticated understanding of the phenomena being studied and serve as a basis for further research.

In this context, case studies were initially designed and written with the aim of serving as the basis for a larger qualitative synthesis. A first round of eight case studies was completed in 2012 with a focus on identifying factors associated with implementation effectiveness, using a minimal framework for investigating and organizing qualitative data that is reflected in the content of the studies. A second round of four indicator-driven case studies was conducted in 2014. As part of the second-phase project design, indicators were discussed, vetted, and revised by researchers involved in the project so that indicators could serve as practical guides for data collection in the case studies. Criterion sampling was thus employed for this study, because all cases focused on the implementation of RTI systems as shaped by legal frameworks, public sector practices, and enabling environments, using a variety of data collection methods for the purposes of triangulation of data, for example, interviews with public officials and civil society organizations, analysis of administrative data, third-party compliance testing and analysis, desk research, and, where possible, use of indicators to structure research and analysis.[16]

Table 1.1 provides details on the sample of cases from a wide variety of contexts. The range of countries studied was limited to some extent by the existence of RTI laws, which are somewhat concentrated in middle- and high-income countries. Most of the countries in the sample passed their RTI laws in the late

Table 1.1 Characteristics of the 12-Country Sample (as of 2014)

Country	Population (millions)	GDP per capita (US$)	State	Government	Political system	Passage of RTI law
Albania	3.2	4,000	Unitary	Parliamentary democracy	Parliamentary	1999
India	1,236.7	1,503	Federal	Federal republic	Parliamentary	2005
Jordan	6.3	4,909	Unitary	Constitutional monarchy	Parliamentary-monarchy	2007
Mexico	120.9	9,749	Federal	Federal republic	Presidential	2002
Moldova	3.6	2,038	Unitary	Republic	Parliamentary	2000
Peru	30.0	6,796	Unitary	Constitutional republic	Presidential	2003
Romania	20.1	8,437	Unitary	Republic	Mixed	2001
South Africa	52.3	7,352	Federal	Republic	Parliamentary	2000
Thailand	66.8	5,480	Unitary	Constitutional monarchy	Parliamentary	1997
Uganda	36.4	551	Unitary	Republic	Mixed	2005
United Kingdom	63.6	38,920	Unitary	Constitutional monarchy	Parliamentary	2000
United States	313.9	51,749	Federal	Federal republic	Presidential	1966

Note: RTI = right to information.

1990s and early 2000s, leading to a timeline of about 10–15 years for implementation at the time of the data collection. Exceptions to this rule are the United States, which passed its in 1966, Uganda in 2005, and Jordan in 2007.

Limitations of Methodology

The data collection and frame for analysis for the underlying case studies were structured by a set of parameters (or indicators) that were informed by prior research and practitioner expertise. However, there is no doubt that some areas could have benefited from a deeper level of inquiry or may have appeared throughout cases even though they were overlooked in the initial data collection instruments. One of the goals of the qualitative analysis was to capture themes and patterns that were not fleshed out in the initial data collection strategy.

The case studies that serve as the basis for this report were researched and written up by a variety of authors, with different levels of focus and knowledge, but with extensive experience in studying or working with RTI systems. They brought different skill sets to the analysis and applied their understandings of what matters for RTI systems to the subject matter, albeit within an analytical framework that required triangulation of data for reliability purposes. Further qualitative or quantitative inquiry into the effectiveness of RTI systems may confirm, clarify, or contradict these findings, but will more than likely build off of the substantial work that has already been accomplished in the case studies.

Because the study is based on only 12 country case studies, the possibility remains that other factors matter for the effectiveness of RTI systems but were not captured in the studies or subsequently in the conclusions. The goal is to highlight findings from the underlying qualitative synthesis as a basis for understanding effective RTI implementation, even if the findings are further refined as additional research is conducted.

Table 1.2 Drivers of Effectiveness in RTI Implementation

1 *Enabling conditions*	2 *Demand for information*	3 *Institutional capacity*	4 *Oversight*

Legal framework
Advocacy efforts
Policy prioritization
	Public awareness and motivation
	Accessibility of RTI processes
		Updated, formal practices
		  Request processing
		  Proactive disclosure
		  Records management
		Staffing levels
		Staff capacity (training and
		  resources)
		Staff incentives
			Monitoring of institutional
			  capacity
			Enforcement of disclosure
			  obligations (appeals,
			  sanctions)

Source: Trapnell and Lemieux 2014.
Note: RTI = right to information.

Domains of Implementation

The nature of the drivers of effectiveness and challenges to effective implementation varies by country. However, based on the underlying research, the drivers can be set out in a heuristic framework comprising *four broad categories* (see table 1.2):

1. Enabling conditions
2. Demand for information
3. Institutional capacity
4. Oversight

This guide discusses each of these four broad categories, their various subcomponents, and how they contribute to effective implementation in greater detail in the following chapters. Appendix B provides a list of key indicators for each of these categories, with recommended sources of evidence that can be used to measure and track RTI effectiveness.

Notes

1. No agreement is in place on the exact number of laws that exist, owing to questions of whether to count laws that have been passed and signed but have not entered into force; it is also affected by different interpretations of the meaning of "countries." For more on this issue, see McIntosh (2011).

2. For more on this aspect of RTI, see chapter 2.

3. For example, the Open Government Partnership makes the existence of an RTI law one of its membership eligibility criteria (see Open Government Partnership 2015).

4. For more information about how RTI laws have been used to achieve development outcomes, see chapter 5.

5. For a discussion on how the ability to control government information gives public officials the ability to exact rents, see Pinto (2009).

6. Information asymmetry occurs where one party has more or better information than the other. This can create an imbalance of power in transactions, which may result in a range of dysfunctions in governance systems (see, for example, Akerlof 1970 and Stigler 1961).

7. The principal-agent theory is commonly used to conceptualize transparency and RTI. See, for example, a discussion of this in Berliner (2014). The concept is also discussed in Dragos, Neamtţu, and Cobârzan (2012), Heald (2006), and Yebezkel (1999).

8. See, for example, Cambridge Economic Associates and PDG South Africa (2014).

9. Some suggest that RTI laws may have unintended negative consequences, such as producing increased public mistrust of government and greater unwillingness of public officials to discuss policy options openly and in a nonpartisan manner. See, for example, Sharma (2015). Sharma argues that use of the RTI laws in India has led to greater public mistrust of government and damaged democracy in India, and another author, Jason Grumet, argues that American government "is more open, more transparent, and less functional than ever before" (see Grumet, Dole, and Daschle 2014). Francis Fukuyama (2014) has said that the United States is in trouble because of "[a]n imbalance between the strength and competence of the state on the one hand, and the institutions that were originally designed to constrain the state on the other." In his latest book, Fukuyama suggests that American democracy has become dysfunctional partly because of excesses in transparency. Too much openness, he worries, has undermined the effectiveness and legitimacy of government (see Fukuyama 2014). This has led to challenges to the value of RTI and greater government openness. Although a full discussion of these issues is outside the scope of this guide, it is likely premature to dismiss the efficacy of RTI laws sui generis, and the openness they are intended to deliver, before the vast majority of these laws have been properly implemented and their impact can be fully evaluated. In spite of some criticisms, RTI is now clearly established as a human right in international law, and establishment and implementation of RTI laws continues to matter.

10. See, for example, RaaG and CES (2014) and Surie and Aiyar (2014).

11. Cobain (2011) reports on Tony Blair's regret at having passed the U.K. FOI Act; see also Blair (2011). In addition, David Cameron has said the FOI "furs up" government arteries (see Associated Press 2012).

12. See, for example, Alexander with McDermott (2014).

13. At time of writing, the South African Human Rights Commission was to be replaced in due course with an information and data protection commission that will have binding powers.

14. Our third degree outcomes also equate to what others describe as impact (see, for example, Calland and Bentley 2013).

15. Themes are identified through iterative coding of the text, and then organized and analyzed for the purpose of interpretation. Reliability is established through intercoder reliability checks on the codes that are generated and the text that is coded, with the aim of assessing the extent to which independent coders reach the same conclusion when evaluating the same text. The purpose of this method is to develop analytical themes through a descriptive synthesis and find explanations relevant to a particular review question.

16. This guide is complemented by three other publications: a volume of the 12 case studies that form the basis for this report (Trapnell 2014), an analysis of data on requests and appeals in eight countries (Lemieux et al. 2015), and a report on the spread of RTI legislation (Mendel 2014).

References

Akerlof, George. 1970. "The Market for 'Lemons': Quality Uncertainty and the Market Mechanism." *Quarterly Journal of Economics* 84 (3): 488–500.

Alexander, Shannon, with Patrice McDermott. 2014. "Implementing Right to Information: A Case Study of the United States." In *Right to Information: Case Studies on Implementation,* edited by Stephanie E. Trapnell, 539–624. Right to Information Series. Washington, DC: World Bank. http://siteresources.worldbank.org/PUBLICSECTOR ANDGOVERNANCE/Resources/285741-1343934891414/8787489-1344020463266 /8788935-1399321576201/RTI_Case_Studies_Implementation_WEBfinal.pdf.

Associated Press. 2012. "David Cameron: FOIs Fur Up Government Arteries." *Huffington Post,* March 6. http://www.huffingtonpost.co.uk/2012/03/06/david-cameron-fois-fur -up_n_1324611.html.

Berliner, Daniel. 2014. "Institutionalizing Transparency: The Global Spread of Freedom of Information Law and Practice." Unpublished PhD dissertation, University of Washington.

Blair, Tony. 2011. *A Journey: My Political Life.* New York: Knopf.

Calland, Richard, and Kristina Bentley. 2013. "The Impact and Effectiveness of Transparency and Accountability Initiatives: Freedom of Information." *Development Policy Review* 31 (S1): s69–87.

Cambridge Economic Associates and PDG South Africa. 2014. "Disclosure of Information in Public Private Partnerships." World Bank Institute, Washington, DC.

Cobain, Iain. 2011. "Mixed Results since Blair's 'Dangerous' Freedom of Information Act Was Launched." *The Guardian,* September 20. http://www.theguardian.com/politics /2011/sep/20/mixed-results-blairs-dangerous-act.

Dragos, Dacian C., Bogdana Neamtţu, and Bianca V. Cobârzan. 2012. "Procedural Transparency in Rural Romania: Linking Implementation with Administrative Capacity?" *International Review of Administrative Sciences* 78 (1): 134–57.

FOIAnet. 2013. "Global Right to Information Update: An Analysis by Region." Freedom of Information Advocates Network. http://foiadvocates.net/?avada_portfolio=global -right-to-information-update-an-analysis-by-region.

Freedominfo.org. 2015. "OGP CSO Leaders Criticize Mexico over FOI Legislation." Freedominfo.org, February 21. http://www.freedominfo.org/2015/02/ogp-cso-leaders -criticize-mexico-over-foi-legislation.

Fukuyama, Francis. 2014. *Political Order and Political Decay: From the Industrial Revolution to the Globalization of Democracy.* New York: Farrar, Straus and Giroux.

Grumet, Jason, Senator Bob Dole, and Senator Tom Daschle. 2014. *City of Rivals: Restoring the Glorious Mess of American Democracy.* Guilford, CT: Lyons Press.

Heald, David. 2006. "Varieties of Transparency." In *Transparency: The Key to Better Governance?* edited by Christopher Hood and David Heald, 25–43. New York: Oxford University Press/British Academy.

Lemieux, Victoria L., Stephanie E. Trapnell, Jesse Worker, and Carole Excel. 2015. "Transparency and Open Government: Reporting on the Disclosure of Information." *JeDEM—eJournal of eDemocracy and Open Government* 7 (2): 75–93. http://www .jedem.org.

McIntosh, Toby. 2011. "FOI Laws: Counts Vary Depending on Definitions." Freedominfo
.org, October 28. http://www.freedominfo.org/2011/10/foi-laws-counts-vary-slightly
-depending-on-definitions.

Mendel, Toby. 2014. *Recent Spread of RTI Legislation*. Right to Information Paper Series.
Washington, DC: World Bank.

Open Government Partnership. 2015. "How It Works: Eligibility Criteria." http://www
.opengovpartnership.org/how-it-works/eligibility-criteria.

Pinto, Juliet. 2009. "Transparency Policy Initiatives in Latin America: Understanding Policy
Outcomes from an Institutional Perspective." *Communication Law and Policy* 14 (1):
41–71.

RaaG (RTI Assessment and Advocacy Group) and CES (Samya Centre for Equity
Studies). 2014. *Peoples' Monitoring of the RTI Regime in India, 2011–2013*. New Delhi:
RaaG and CES.

Sharma, Prashant. 2015. *Democracy and Transparency in the Indian State: The Making of
the Right to Information Act*. New York: Routledge.

Stigler, George J. 1961. "The Economics of Information." *Journal of Political Economy*
69 (3): 213–25.

Surie, Mandakini Devasher, and Yamini Aiyar. 2014. "Implementing Right to Information:
A Case Study of India." In *Right to Information: Case Studies on Implementation*,
edited by Stephanie E. Trapnell, 49–102. Right to Information Series. Washington,
DC: World Bank. http://siteresources.worldbank.org/PUBLICSECTORAND
GOVERNANCE/Resources/285741-1343934891414/8787489-1344020463266
/8788935-1399321576201/RTI_Case_Studies_Implementation_WEBfinal.pdf.

Trapnell, Stephanie E., ed. 2014. *Right to Information: Case Studies on Implementation*.
Right to Information Series. Washington, DC: World Bank. http://siteresources
.worldbank.org/PUBLICSECTORANDGOVERNANCE/Resources/285741
-1343934891414/8787489-1344020463266/8788935-1399321576201/RTI_Case
_Studies_Implementation_WEBfinal.pdf.

Trapnell, Stephanie E., and Victoria L. Lemieux. 2014. "Right to Information: Identifying
Drivers of Effectiveness in Implementation." Right to Information Working
Paper Series 2. World Bank, Washington, DC. http://siteresources.worldbank.org
/PUBLICSECTORANDGOVERNANCE/Resources/285741-1343934891414
/8787489-1344020463266/8788935-1399321576201/RTI_Drivers_of_Effectiveness
_WP2_26Nov2014.pdf.

Worker, Jesse, with Carole Excell. 2014. "Requests and Appeals Data in Right to
Information Systems: Brazil, India, Jordan, Mexico, South Africa, Thailand, United
Kingdom, and United States." Working Paper, World Bank, Washington, DC. http://
siteresources.worldbank.org/PUBLICSECTORANDGOVERNANCE/Resources
/285741-1343934891414/8787489-1344020463266/8788935-1399321576201
/Requests_and_Appeals_RTI_Working_Paper.pdf.

World Bank. 2013. "Freedom of Information Systems: A Background Primer." Public Sector
and Governance Group, Public Accountability Mechanisms Initiative, World Bank.
https://agidata.org/Pam/Documents/FOI%20Primer_30Sep2013.pdf.

Yebezkel, Dror. 1999. "Transparency and Openness of Quality Democracy." In *Openness
and Transparency in Governance: Challenges and Opportunities*, edited by Michael
Kelly, 25–43. Maastricht: NISPAcee Forum.

CHAPTER 2

Legal Frameworks for RTI

Section 1: History and Development of RTI Laws

A review of the history and development of right to information (RTI) laws provides useful background to a discussion of the effective implementation of these laws. In particular, it is important to understand that some of the broad social, technological, and political drivers that have contributed to the emergence of RTI laws also continue to shape the enabling environment for their implementation.

The predecessor to the RTI laws of today—arguably the first RTI law—was the 1766 Swedish government law on Fundamental Rights and Freedoms, which embedded a right to information for the general public in the Swedish constitution and granted specific rights to information to the press.[1] Passage of the Swedish law was followed by a Finnish law in 1951 after a long hiatus, followed by a law in the United States in 1966 and laws in Denmark and Norway in 1970, France and the Netherlands in 1978, Australia and New Zealand in 1982, and Canada in 1983. Among developing countries, Colombia was the first to pass an RTI law, in 1985 (Mendel 2009). The next wave of laws to be passed outside of the developed world were in Eastern Europe, with Hungary and Ukraine both passing them in 1992 (Berliner 2012). In the period between passage of the Swedish law and the mid-1990s, fewer than 20 RTI laws existed (Holsen and Pasquier 2012, 216). From that time onward, however, the pace of growth in RTI laws has been remarkable, with the number of national RTI laws increasing from 19 mostly Western democracies in 1995 to about 100 laws in all regions of the world today (see map 2.1).

Even as the number of countries with RTI laws has rapidly increased, passage of the laws has been an exercise requiring stamina in many countries. It has taken some countries extended periods between when an RTI was first recognized in a national constitution or was first discussed and actual passage of the law. In Uganda, for example, there was a 10-year gap between adoption of the constitutional guarantee of the RTI in 1995 and passage of an RTI act in 2005. In the United Kingdom, after a civil society campaign dating back to at least 1984, and after many years of promising an RTI law, a law was finally passed in 2000, but it was not brought fully into force until 2005 (Berliner 2012, 7). In India, the gap

Map 2.1 National Laws and Regulations on Public Access to Information, Including RTI Laws, Showing Countries with Some Legislative Guarantee of Public Access to Information (Shaded) and Those Countries with No Legislative Guarantees (Not Shaded)

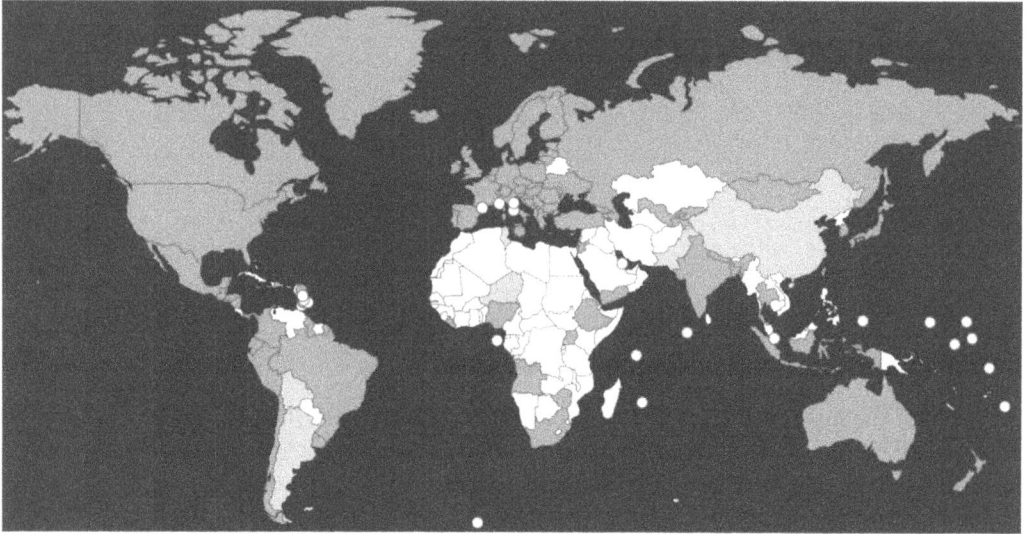

Source: Article 19, Mapping Project.
Note: The darker the shading the greater the legislative guarantee of public access to information. For current ratings and to explore an interactive map of RTI laws by country go to http://www.article19.org/maps/. RTI = right to information.

between the Supreme Court's recognition of the RTI as being contained in the constitution and passage of the law was more than 20 years.

What accounts for the recent rapid uptick in the passage of RTI laws? A number of interrelated factors have been cited in the literature on RTI. These can be grouped broadly into two interacting and mutually reinforcing categories. First, there are factors exogenous to a country, such as pressure from international organizations or transnational nongovernmental actors, as well as the evolution of transparency in general, and RTI in particular, as a global norm. Broader social, political, and technological trends have also influenced passage of laws. Second, there are endogenous factors, such as lobbying by local actors, political transition (e.g., during processes of democratization), and increased political competition. We now turn to a consideration of each of these factors in turn.

Exogenous Factors

International organizations and networks have played an important role in the spread of RTI laws, especially in postconflict and less well-resourced countries, through the application of direct pressure and/or through transmission of regional or global norms. In Eastern and Central European countries, for example, RTI laws grew, in part, out of pressure from Western Europe to pass RTI laws as a condition of entry into the European Union (Mendel 2014). Similarly, international policy networks, such as the Open Government Partnership (OGP), which bases countries' eligibility for membership in part on whether they have an RTI law, have also influenced passage of these laws (Open Government

Partnership 2015). International aid agencies have often played a role in RTI adoption. The Organization of American States (OAS), for instance, supported the development and adoption of RTI legislation throughout Latin America (Mendel 2014). Active civil society campaigns, such as the International Right to Know Day and strategic litigation, backed up by an increasingly influential global civil society movement for RTI, have also helped create strong pressure for the introduction of RTI laws.[2] International ratings and assessments of a country have provided a further impetus in some countries (e.g., in Uganda and Sudan).[3] Taken together, these international dynamics have established global norms of openness and transparency that, ultimately, have contributed to passage of RTI laws in many countries (Dokeniya 2014b; Florini 1999; Roberts 2006).

Less direct influence in a number of cases in recent times has come from growing recognition of access to information in public bodies as a fundamental human right. Arguably, this has been particularly true in Latin America, where there has been important human rights rulings, and in Africa, where an African Charter on Human and Peoples' Rights has been recognized in six African Union treaties (FOIAnet 2013, 15). The original guarantees of freedom of expression found in the Universal Declaration on Human Rights and the International Covenant on Civil and Political Rights (ICCPR) refer to the right to "impart" information and ideas as well as the right to "seek" and "receive" information. One of the earliest authoritative statements to the effect that this formulation included the RTI is found in the 1998 annual report of the UN Special Rapporteur on the promotion and protection of the right to freedom of opinion and expression to the United Nations Commission on Human Rights, in which he stated: "[T]he right to seek, receive and impart information imposes a positive obligation on States to ensure access to information, particularly with regard to information held by Government in all types of storage and retrieval systems" (Mendel 2014; United Nations OHCHR 1998, 4). RTI has since been given formal international legal recognition, first by the Inter-American Court of Human Rights in the 2006 case of *Claude Reyes and Others v. Chile* and then, in 2009, by the European Court of Human Rights, with the UN Commission on Human Rights, clearly recognizing the RTI in its 2011 General Comment on Article 19 of the ICCPR (Mendel 2014). The most obvious manifestation of this trend has been a subtle shift in the title of laws providing access to information held by public bodies from "freedom of information" or "access to information" laws to calling them "right to information laws." In principle, governments that signed up to international conventions were bound to give effect to those principles in national laws (Dokeniya 2014b, 36; Roberts 2006).

Citizens have demanded, and governments have increasingly recognized, the importance of openness as part of the democratic state-citizen compact.[4] Taking root over the same period as the rise of RTI laws has been a growing call from citizens in democratic states or states undergoing processes of democratization for more open, accountable, and participatory government (see, for example, Carothers and Brechenmacher 2014). Open and participatory government has emerged as a global norm that has been institutionalized by a number of national and transnational organizational actors, such as the OGP. It is therefore not surprising to observe a rough correlation between the presence of RTI laws and more robust democracies. Indeed, Mendel notes that processes of democratic transition often have been accompanied by early demand for the adoption of an RTI law (Mendel 2014). Such processes also are reflected in the increasing number of RTI laws that include provisions for proactive disclosure of information (Darbishire 2010).[5]

Reflecting the broad rise in citizen demand for greater openness, citizens have taken action in recent years to demand greater transparency and accountability in countries that have recently emerged from repressive regimes (e.g., Tunisia in the wake of the Arab Spring). Closely intertwined with these demands has been a global trend toward wider access to information via Internet-based technologies and mobile platforms, which, as Mendel observes, has made it easier for citizens in these countries to learn about the benefits of RTI even when the use of these technologies has been subject to restrictive measures.[6] These dynamics have created pressure to introduce measures that provide greater transparency and accountability, which in some cases has been manifested in passage of an RTI law. New laws in Tunisia (2011) and the Republic of Yemen (2012) and the possibility of laws in Morocco and the Arab Republic of Egypt at the time of writing provide examples representative of this trend.

Endogenous Factors

Dokeniya notes that, in several countries, pro-reform coalitions of ruling and opposition parties, civil society groups, and media reduced opposition or resistance to passage of an RTI law (Dokeniya 2013, 2014b, 1). At the same time, as Mendel observes, in various countries—such as Brazil, Indonesia, and Nigeria—it has taken a long time to enact laws despite strong civil society advocacy. Longstanding campaigns in other countries, including Ghana, Malaysia, and the Philippines, also have yet to bear fruit (Mendel 2014). This suggests that civil society advocacy alone is not enough to ensure passage of RTI laws; there also must be at least some support from those in political power. This has been the case in countries, such as those in Eastern and Central Europe, where reformist-minded politicians led processes of democratization.

A number of writers suggest that democratization processes in Central and Eastern Europe and other parts of the world drove passage of RTI laws from the early 1990s to the 2000s (see, for example, Mendel 2014). Mendel, for instance, finds that, in the wake of the revolutions in Central and Eastern Europe in the 1990s and democratization processes in other regions, the rate of passage of RTI laws was five times more than what it had been up to that point. In Eastern Europe, 20 countries adopted RTI laws, representing nearly one-half of all of the new laws adopted during the 10-year period following the collapse of the Soviet Union (Mendel 2014). Similarly, Indonesia and Thailand (1997), following periods of economic collapse, political renewal, and a new constitution; South Africa (2000); the United Kingdom (2000), following a change of government after 17 years of rule by the same party; Mexico (2002), following a change of government after 65 years of rule by the same party; and

Uganda (2005) and Nigeria (2011) as part of a struggle for democratic rights all provide examples of the influence that democratic processes have had on the growth of RTI laws (Mendel, 2014; FOIAnet 2013, 18). Berliner, on the other hand, argues that many so-called reformist leaders who promised to pass RTI laws when they came to power failed to do so or delayed passage of the laws for lengthy periods (Berliner 2012).

Other writers find that different political systems have influenced the passage of RTI laws. McClean, for example, argues that countries with developed democracies and political competition or presidential systems are more likely to lead to transparency measures, such as passage of RTI laws (McClean 2011). Berliner points to increased political uncertainty rather than political transition or the type of political system as a better explanation of why political actors pass RTI laws. He argues that RTI laws act as a kind of insurance policy for political elites when they see that they may lose political power. As an example, he points to the Republic of Korea's law, which was first introduced in July 1996 by the New Korea Party under Kim Young-sam but passed only in December 1996 when the ruling party lost its parliamentary majority but before it lost power completely (Berliner 2012). Brian Levy's argument that transparency is a governance intervention best suited to more competitive political systems echoes the arguments advanced by both McClean and Berliner (Levy 2014).

Consideration of diverse theories explaining the evolution of RTI laws can help us reflect upon whether the laws are, for example, one of the following:

- The outcome of political pressure on reluctant political actors, characterized as either being without sufficient internal political strength to resist such pressure (Michener 2011) or seeing sufficient gain in obtaining regional or international legitimacy that they are willing to give up some degree of control over information[7]
- The result of the spread of global norms (e.g., of openness, transparency, citizen participation, and human rights) aided by availability and use of information and communication technologies
- The outcome of lobbying and pressure from local civil society actors (Dokeniya 2014b)
- The result of democratization processes or similar political transitions (Mendel 2014)
- An association with a particular type of state (McClean 2011)
- A form of political insurance in the context of increased internal political competition (Berliner 2012)

Greater understanding of the dynamics of the passage of RTI laws not only helps to explain why and how such laws come into being in particular contexts, but also potentially to aid reformers seeking to pass a law in another country. In addition, such understanding strengthens our awareness of what forces may prevent subsequent efforts to weaken or retract RTI laws. In the final analysis, there is likely no single causal factor that explains passage of RTI laws in all cases;

rather, all of the dynamics discussed in this chapter have tended to work in various combinations to generate the conditions that allow for passage of an RTI law in a given country context.

Section 2: Designing RTI Laws for Effective Implementation

From the historical evolution and factors leading to the passage of RTI laws, we now turn to a discussion of the legal provisions that make up these laws, noting that a sound legal design can help to reduce the noticeable gap that exists in many countries between what RTI laws specify about the disclosure of information and the extent to which laws are actually implemented and functioning in practice to disclose information. The design of effective RTI laws is a complex issue to which justice cannot be done in one brief chapter. Readers are therefore referred to a much fuller treatment of the topic in the report *Designing Right to Information Laws for Effective Implementation* upon which this chapter is based (Mendel 2015).

We agree with Richard Calland that the time to think about implementation of an RTI law is not when it is passed, but at the time of drafting. He argues that provisions of the law need to be drafted so as to anticipate implementation challenges, such as whether there will be resistance. He cites the case of South Africa, where both the legislative committee and the South African civil society pressure group—the Open Democracy Campaign Group—saw the need for a higher level of specificity when drafting provisions relating to procedures and systems to more easily hold government departments to account for implementation (Calland 2003). This chapter therefore discusses the different areas where better or more careful legal design might reduce the burden on public authorities and others tasked with implementing RTI while, at the same time, retaining the robustness of those laws. It addresses provisions in both the RTI law and the subordinate legislation, such as regulations, that complement the law and are easier to amend.

Integration of RTI Laws into Planning Processes and Preexisting Laws

In the drafting of RTI laws, the issue of bureaucratic integration and fit requires attention to ensure fluid integration of RTI obligations into internal bureaucratic systems. RTI is not likely to be successful if it is not integrated into major planning processes relating to budgeting, human resource allocation, and other public sector management systems. Without proper integration, public agencies may be left without public information officers/units to respond to requests, or these officers/units will be without resources to perform their duties. Consideration also must be given to structural features (e.g., how the information officers/units are formally designated and their relationship with the rest of the public authority) as well as incentives and sanctions. In order for information officers/units to perform their duties effectively, it is important that the responsibilities and powers of the information officer function be defined clearly, the job description of the function be set out, and its place within the bureaucracy and the obligations of other officers to cooperate with it in identifying and finding information be defined clearly.

Another key consideration is the range of preexisting laws, rules, and regulations. In many cases, the regulatory framework establishing RTI and ensuring its implementation consists of several laws, decrees, or ministerial orders, some of which contradict the principle of disclosure, and some of which support RTI through implementing rules.

Many countries either have state secrets laws that supersede or are treated as dominating RTI laws[8] or have RTI laws with broad exemptions to disclosure, making it difficult for officials to determine what kinds of information can be disclosed, particularly if they are penalized for violating exemption requirements. This can discourage information disclosure. For example, in some cases, archives laws contain outdated secrecy provisions that contradict RTI laws. Employment contracts, which may have been designed some time ago, can also impose broad duties of secrecy on civil servants. In other cases, internal codes of conduct may include rules on secrecy, and there may well be other internal organizational rules or systems that do the same, making it difficult for public information officers to transition to greater disclosure of information even when the RTI law allows it.

Better integration of RTI laws and fewer conflicts with other laws is more likely to be achieved in contexts that emphasize good regulatory practices (GRPs). GRPs enhance the quality of regulatory regimes and their outcomes and put in place effective, transparent, accountable, and consultative reform processes that assist in reform prioritization, design, and implementation.[9]

Provisions Governing Definitions and Scope

For certain provisions of RTI laws, a direct causal relationship is found between the rules and how RTI regimes are implemented and function to disclose information in practice. These include provisions specifying definitions and the scope of the laws, the regime of exemptions established in law, and the procedures for processing requests. In these areas, it is necessary to ensure clarity of terms and introduce well-articulated provisions relating to the scope of a law's application, because doing so will naturally limit the administrative discretion that has to be applied when implementing the law. Vaguely worded laws also allow for greater administrative decision making to implement, which "can lead to differential application by different public authorities, undermining public confidence and generating unmet expectations, and can also provide opportunities for abuse of that discretion to prevent disclosure of information" (Mendel 2015, 30).[10] Moreover, discretion is costly and places a burden on officials, since they may have to verify information such as the citizenship of requestors or make decisions on whether certain types of information fall within the scope of a law.

Some countries have crafted legal provisions that reduce the need for administrative discretion. These provisions include avoiding qualifications of the definition of information in ways that would require officials to consider whether the qualification has been met; extending the right to access information to everyone, not just residents or citizens, so that officials do not need to verify residency or citizenship; and providing a list of examples of the types of situations where the public interest might override exemptions.

Provisions on Central Support Bodies

The design of legal provisions concerning central support bodies is also an important determinant of how well RTI laws function in practice. These central bodies include both internal government support bodies (nodal agencies) and external support bodies (independent administrative oversight bodies and courts). There are three main roles undertaken by these bodies: (1) supporting internal government institutional capacity for implementation, (2) dealing with complaints, and (3) raising public awareness and support. Each of these roles is critical to the effective operation of RTI regimes. Often less recognized but still of critical importance is the role of the central body that provides support to the usually hundreds of separate public agencies responsible for developing systems to support implementation of RTI laws (Mendel 2015). In many cases, public agencies charged with responding to requests lack the expertise to develop effective rules and systems on their own. Even where they are able to do so, requiring each agency to develop its own approach absent a central coordinating body frequently leads to uneven approaches to implementation of the law, which can reduce effectiveness. A strong central support body can alleviate these problems and relieve part of the burden on individual agencies for establishment of rules and systems (e.g., tracking systems) to support implementation of RTI. Specification in laws of responsibility for these roles, legal establishment of the central support bodies designated as performing these roles, and careful attention to institutional design and role allocation options in the development of RTI laws can provide a basis for identifying the need for resources to carry out these functions, ensure their continued existence, and, ultimately, help prevent systemic failures during implementation.

Provisions on Oversight and Enforcement

In many jurisdictions, enforcement provisions of RTI laws are very weak. Typically, the rules on responding to requests for information are clearly set out in the provisions of RTI laws, and provisions address how to appeal any denials of, or failures to process, requests (e.g., breach of timelines, etc.), beginning with an appeal to the administrative body to which a request is initially submitted, often followed by appeal to an oversight body, such as an information commissioner, and progressing all the way to the courts in many countries. In other areas of RTI laws, however, the rules regarding oversight and enforcement are much less clear. Rules relating to proactive disclosure, for instance, are often much weaker than for responsive disclosure, with no provisions concerning oversight and enforcement and no provision for increasing disclosure over time to ensure that laws remain current.

Provisions concerning oversight and enforcement of records management practices are, similarly, often absent from RTI laws, possibly because of a sense that oversight and enforcement of records management is dealt with sufficiently in archival or public records laws when, in fact, this may not be the case. Even when archival or public records laws do address records management, these laws usually do not establish independent oversight and enforcement provisions and thus could be strengthened by the inclusion of provisions allowing for such oversight through the RTI law. In drafting RTI laws, there is a need to establish oversight and enforcement mechanisms for all essential components of RTI regimes, including appointment of information officers, proactive disclosure of information, and records management.

There is also a need for a stronger role for independent oversight bodies, such as information commissioners, to enable them, for example, to undertake independent studies on how certain aspects of the law are functioning in practice, establish binding standards relating to critical areas of operation affecting the RTI laws, such as records management, conduct investigations when necessary, and issue orders to address implementation gaps.

No law is ever perfectly implemented, but the gap between RTI policy and practice has historically been quite significant. This chapter has discussed several ways that careful legal design may facilitate more effective implementation. Attention to good legal design has the potential to reduce the policy-practice gap that has arisen in many jurisdictions. Strategies for effective legal design include reducing administrative discretion by drafting clear and simple rules, drafting provisions that establish and clearly define the role of central support bodies and strengthen oversight and enforcement, and drafting legal provisions that pay careful attention to the way in which the RTI rules and systems are integrated into bureaucratic planning and regulatory systems. The latter entails consideration of the RTI law in relation to sanctions and disclosure and/or secrecy provisions in other laws and reviewing how the RTI law fits into the broader policy framework of the country.

Section 3: Privacy, Secrecy, and Openness

As discussed in the previous section, the legal design of exemption provisions will have a significant impact upon effective implementation of RTI in a given context. Among the most important and complex of exemption provisions are those relating to privacy or secrecy. In considering the best approach, there is always a balance to be struck between disclosure and nondisclosure. Laws providing a right of access to information held in public bodies can have many positive benefits; however, in some cases, excessive openness has the potential to cause harm to individuals or to work against the public interest. This is true, in particular, where access to information conflicts with the right to personal privacy or national security, which are among the more complex exceptions to the right of access. For this reason, RTI laws almost always include exemption provisions relating to protection of privacy and security. Alternatively, privacy and security may be protected in separate laws.[11]

It is a difficult task to resolve the tensions that frequently arise between disclosure and nondisclosure. A judge or information commissioner applying the law, a legislator drafting criteria into a law or regulation, or a public official applying the law in the absence of detailed exemption provisions may have to do so, however. How do these public officials strike the right balance (see, for example, box 2.1)? These issues have become paramount, and decision making therefore more complex, in light of the fact that digital technologies and massive data storage capacity have changed the dynamic between openness and privacy.[12] Given the potential impact of decisions about disclosure of information on citizens' trust of the state, it is important to carefully consider how to strike the right balance between disclosure and nondisclosure.[13]

Significant potential remains for conflicts between privacy and openness, however, as the story in box 2.2 indicates, because striking the right balance between information disclosure, on the one hand, and protecting privacy and secrecy, on the other hand, outside of the consideration of specific laws and legal provisions that provide guidance to decision makers is so often a question of context. Nevertheless, principles can be identified in the next section, that public officials can rely upon to guide their decision making in the absence of specific legal frameworks, such as those provided by well-defined RTI exemption provisions.

Balancing Disclosure and Privacy

In case of conflict between RTI and the right to privacy, neither right necessarily has greater weight in international law, though how they are treated by the courts in practice in individual countries will vary from country to country and change over time.[14] In cases of conflict, however, the decision maker may have to rely upon a public interest balancing test when determining whether information should be disclosed. This applies to all classes of exemptions, not only to exemptions on the basis of privacy. An example of such a public interest test is presented in the case described in box 2.2. Under a public interest balancing test, even if the information is determined to be personal and its release would cause harm to an individual, it may be disclosed if it is found that the public interest in release is more important than the potential harm that could be caused to the individual. This allows for the decision maker, in the absence of a specific legal framework, to weigh the different values and determine, case by case, when information should be released (Banisar 2011, 18).

Box 2.1 Balancing Disclosure with Nondisclosure

In Canada recently, the government blacked out the name of visiting British Prime Minister David Cameron from various documents relating to his visit. The basis for this was that the information was private, even though the functions were public functions that had been open to the media (with pictures having been published). This example illustrates the tensions that can arise between protection of privacy and providing public access to information.

Source: Centre for Law and Democracy and Africa Freedom of Information Centre 2014, 15.

Box 2.2 Example of Application of a Public Interest Test

Mersey Tunnel Users' Association v. Information Commissioner and Merseytravel (EA/2007/0052, February 15, 2008) concerned a request for legal advice received by Merseytravel, which operates the Mersey tunnels. Merseytravel had previously met losses on operating the tunnels by increasing the levy on the Merseyside district councils. When the tunnels started to make a profit the issue arose as to whether the profit should be used to repay the councils (treating the levy increase as a loan) or whether it could be used to reduce toll charges. After getting legal advice, Merseytravel used the money to repay the councils. The advice was legally privileged, and hence FOIA section 42 was engaged. This is a qualified exemption, so the question was whether the public interest in maintaining legal privilege outweighed the public interest in disclosure. The balance of public interest, as described by the Information Tribunal, can be summarized as follows:

Public interest in maintaining the exemption

- The significant inbuilt weight of public interest in maintaining legal privilege. The Tribunal said that the inbuilt weight would have been even greater if the advice had significantly affected individuals.
- The advice was still "live," in the sense that it was still being relied on.

Public interest in disclosure

- The specific need for transparency in this case because of Merseytravel's lack of clarity about their legal duty to repay the district councils, in addition to the general public interest in transparency.
- The amount of money involved (tens of millions of pounds)
- The numbers of people affected (all users of the tunnels)
- The age of the information (it was 14 years old) diminished the impact on legal privilege and reduced the weight of the argument for the exemption.

The outcome depended on the relative weight of the arguments on each side, not the quantity of those arguments. The Information Tribunal said at paragraph 51: "Weighed in the round, and considering all the aspects discussed above, we are not persuaded that the public interest in maintaining the exemption is as weighty as in the other cases considered by the Tribunal; and in the opposing scales, the factors that favor disclosure are not just equally weighty, they are heavier."

Source: Banisar 2011, 13.
Note: FOIA = Freedom of Information Act.

As an example, the Slovenian information commissioner has identified areas where there would be a strong argument in favor of disclosure on the grounds of public interest. These exist in one or more of the following cases:

- The disclosure will assist public understanding of an issue of current national debate;
- The issue has generated public or parliamentary debate;

- Proper debate cannot take place without wide availability of all relevant information;
- An issue affects a wide range of individuals or companies;
- The issue affects public safety or public health;
- The release of information would promote accountability and transparency in decision making;
- The issue concerns the making or spending of public money (Banisar 2011, 20–21).

Recent European decisions about disclosure of information relating to public figures points to a growing trend toward disclosure of their financial information in spite of privacy considerations.[15] In 2007 the European Ombudsman found that it was maladministration for the European parliament to refuse to disclose the expenses of members of parliament, including their travel and subsistence allowances. The Irish and U.K. information commissions have also ordered the release of parliamentary members' expense information, and all U.S. congressional expenditures are published biannually (Banisar 2011, 13). Some general principles regarding disclosure of personal information of public officials that have emerged can be summarized as follows (Banisar 2011):

- *Official capacities*—The majority of countries take the position that most information relating to official capacities is not considered personal information for the purposes of nondisclosure. Generally, documents cannot be withheld just because an official's name is listed as the author or recipient.
- *Employment information*—There appears to be no consensus on information related to an official's performance in his or her job (including exact salary and details of employee performance reviews, although salary bands linked to individuals are often provided). Such information is withheld in many jurisdictions and is available in others.
- *Personal life*—Information relating solely to a public employee's personal life rather than to his or her public actions is less likely to be released. Medical records of nonelected officials are generally considered sensitive and are not released in any system. In some cases, the medical records of very high-ranking officials (such as a president) may be publicly released in the public interest. For nonelected officials, criminal records not related to their positions are often withheld.
- *Elected or high-ranking officials*—Notwithstanding the above, there is also significant agreement that information about elected or high-ranking public officials should be less restricted, even when it relates to their personal lives. In India, for example, the Supreme Court has ruled that the criminal records of persons running for parliament should be released. Biographical data of decision makers and those who are being considered for very senior positions are more commonly released than those for more junior positions.

These decisions reflect a gradual spread of global norms favoring disclosure of information relating to high or elected officials. Each country, however, will have its own particular stance on what it considers an appropriate balance, and, in some cases, this stance may be far from the norms discussed above.

Balancing Disclosure and Secrecy for Reasons of National Security

Turning to the question of balancing disclosure with the need to protect national security interests, the Tshwane Principles on National Security and the Right to Information offer guidance (Centre for Law and Democracy 2015; Open Society Justice Initiative 2013). These principles are based on international, regional, and national law; standards; good practices; and the writings of experts. Fifteen of the main points of the Tshwane Principles[16] are as follows:

1. The public has a right of access to government information, including information from private entities that perform public functions or receive public funds. (Principle 1)
2. It is up to the government to prove the necessity of restrictions on RTI. (Principle 4)
3. Governments may legitimately withhold information in narrowly defined areas, such as defense plans, weapons development, and the operations and sources used by intelligence services. Also, they may withhold confidential information supplied by foreign governments that is linked to national security matters. (Principle 9)
4. But governments should never withhold information concerning violations of international human rights and humanitarian law, including information about the circumstances and perpetrators of torture and crimes against humanity, and the location of secret prisons. This includes information about past abuses under previous regimes and any information they hold regarding violations committed by their own agents or by others. (Principle 10A)
5. The public has a right to know about systems of surveillance and the procedures for authorizing them. (Principle 10E)
6. No government entity may be exempt from disclosure requirements—including the security sector and intelligence authorities. The public also has a right to know about the existence of all security sector entities, the laws and regulations that govern them, and their budgets. (Principles 5 and 10C)
7. Whistleblowers in the public sector should not face retaliation if the public interest in the information disclosed outweighs the public interest in secrecy. But they should have first made a reasonable effort to address the issue through official complaint mechanisms, provided that an effective mechanism exists. (Principles 40, 41, and 43)
8. Criminal action against those who leak information should be considered only if the information poses a "real and identifiable risk of causing significant harm" that overrides the public interest in disclosure. (Principles 43 and 46)

9. Journalists and others who do not work for the government should not be prosecuted for receiving, possessing, or disclosing classified information to the public, or for conspiracy or other crimes based on their seeking or accessing classified information. (Principle 47)

10. Journalists and others who do not work for the government should not be forced to reveal a confidential source or other unpublished information in a leak investigation. (Principle 48)

11. Public access to judicial processes is essential: "invocation of national security may not be relied upon to undermine the fundamental right of the public to access judicial processes." Media and the public should be permitted to challenge any limitation on public access to judicial processes. (Principle 28)

12. Governments should not be permitted to keep state secrets or other information confidential that prevents victims of human rights violations from seeking or obtaining a remedy for their violation. (Principle 30)

13. There should be independent oversight bodies for the security sector, and the bodies should be able to access all information needed for effective oversight. (Principles 6, 31–33)

14. Information should be classified only as long as necessary and never indefinitely. Laws should govern the maximum permissible period of classification. (Principle 16)

15. There should be clear procedures for requesting declassification, with priority procedures for the declassification of information of public interest. (Principle 17)

Balancing Disclosure and Openness

The Tshwane Principles articulate international norms with respect to balancing disclosure and nondisclosure in the context of national security interests. However, as in the case of balancing privacy with openness, countries often diverge from these norms and apply their own standards.

Wherever discretionary decision making is applied, there is room for politics, culture, and even individual cognitive bias to play a role in determining the outcome. Exemption provisions, including those that protect personal privacy and national security interests, can be misused—used to cover up or benefit vested interests unfairly—rather than being used as intended to protect the rights of individuals or the public interest. In Argentina and the United Kingdom, the government has, in the past, claimed that information about officials' expenses is personal information, with the result that such information remained closed.[17] In such cases, a well-functioning independent oversight body[18] is crucial, as such a body can monitor application of exemption provisions, receive complaints, scrutinize decision making, and bring pressure to bear when decision making is not in accordance with the law, related procedures and principles, or even, in some cases, global norms. Active and free media and civil society groups also can bring pressure to bear for greater openness, as has been the case in the United Kingdom around disclosure of information about officials' expenses.

In other cases, public officials may be applying provisions and making decisions in a context of long-standing traditions of secrecy, in some countries buttressed by laws, such as official secrets acts, which may not have been repealed with the introduction of an RTI law. In these contexts, subtle, and not so subtle, influences on the official decision maker may tilt decision making in favor of nondisclosure. Again, strong, independent oversight bodies can help to gradually shift decision making in favor of new levels of disclosure through training and rulings on complaints. The tone from the central government and government incentive structures will also have an important role to play in overcoming long traditions of government secrecy and in ensuring that an appropriate balance exists between disclosure and nondisclosure.

Individual cognitive biases can also play a role. These can be a factor whenever there is some discretionary aspect to decision making, which is often unavoidable in the application of RTI exemption provisions given the need to balance competing rights and interests. Cognitive biases can lead to systematic deviations from rational or principled decisions and arise from the way in which individual decision makers simplify decision making by applying heuristics—using their experience to form mental guidelines for their decisions—as well as their personal motivations and expectations.[19] For example, FOIAnet has observed that, in various African states where liberation movements have overthrown oppressive authoritarian regimes, the members of these movements—now government officials—have relied upon secrecy to conduct their operations against former dictatorships (FOIAnet 2013, 16–17). As a result, secrecy has become like a "mental operating system" that has proved difficult to overcome once these liberators form new governments. FOIAnet also observes that cognitive biases can intertwine with secretive cultures left by former colonial regimes to further dilute efforts to open up government (FOIAnet 2013, 17).

Evidence also suggests that citizenry may be a factor too. Case studies on RTI in Eastern and Central Europe and in Africa suggest that years of oppression can leave citizens with a residual fear of demanding RTI.[20] Moreover, citizens may also feel indebted to liberators and therefore reluctant to press them to disclose information (FOIAnet 2013, 16). For this reason, it is important to raise awareness among members of society and civil society groups about balancing privacy and secrecy with openness as well as to do so among public officials. Consistent with the notion that RTI regimes operate as systems of interconnected components, RTI laws work best if all components—in this case institutional capacity and demand for information—are equally developed. It is to a discussion of the interlocking components of effective RTI implementation that we now turn.

Notes

1. Holsen and Pasquier (2012); Kingdom of Sweden, Fundamental Rights and Freedoms (1766), Freedom of the Press Act (1766). See http://www.chydenius.net/pdf/worlds _first_foia.pdf.

2. See, for example, Freedom of Information Advocates Network (FOIAnet), http://
foiadvocates.net. In their 2013 "Global Right to Information Update" (FOIAnet 2013,
10), they make specific reference to seeking "to foster better understanding and to
stimulate international dialogue among the different regions of the world about this
core human rights issue and its development . . . the update also aims to draw attention to the global nature of the movement for the right to information."

3. Baitarian (2015); Dokeniya (2014a, 37).

4. For more on government accountability mechanisms and their relationship to openness, see *World Development Report 2004: Making Services Work for Poor People* (World
Bank 2004).

5. Note that a number of countries (e.g., the United States) also have open data laws that
cover proactive disclosure of information.

6. Mendel (2014). Dokeniya also observes that "Over the last two decades or so, transparency has emerged as a powerful idea in discourses on governance and development.
Undoubtedly, rapid developments in information and communications technologies
have played an important role in this. The technology to share and process information
at unprecedented speeds has massively increased information flows, fundamentally
changed cultures around information, and heighten[ed] citizen expectations of what
they are entitled to know about the function of the government (Dokeniya 2014b, 33).

7. As in South Sudan.

8. The relationship between RTI and state secrecy laws is often legally unclear; thus,
secrecy laws are treated as dominating because of stronger incentives to comply.

9. For more on good regulatory practices, see OECD (2015).

10. For example, discretionary interpretation of provisions in RTI laws can lead to a quite
different disclosure of information; see Open Society Justice Initiative (2006).

11. For example, the Canadian province of British Columbia, Hungary, Mexico, and
Thailand each has a single combined RTI and privacy law. The United Kingdom has a
separate Data Protection Act. For a map of data protection laws around the world, see
http://www.privacyinternational.org/survey/dpmap.jpg. For a fuller discussion of the
various models, see Banisar (2011, ch. 3). In addition, there is also sectoral legislation
applying to health, financial, and credit records; some telecommunications records;
educational records; and other areas at both the national and state levels. For a comprehensive overview, see Solove and Schwartz (2008).

12. For a discussion of some of the concerns raised by digital technologies coupled with
massive data storage capacity, discussions of the revelations of Edward Snowden
around the data collection practices of the U.S. National Security Agency can be cited
as an example (e.g., Greenwald 2013). Collection and storage of personal information
in many countries has been prompted by rising security concerns. For a detailed discussion of these developments see, for example, United Nations OHCHR (2014) and
Centre for Law and Democracy (2015).

13. The relationship between disclosure (transparency) and citizens' trust of the state is
not an uncomplicated one. Transparency advocates have often argued that it increases
citizen trust; however, there is evidence to suggest that it may have the opposite effect
(see, for example, Peixoto 2013). The point is arguably not whether it increases or
decreases citizens' trust in any particular case, but whether—much like the operation
of the rule of law—it introduces a transparent and fair process and an important governance capability (in the case of RTI, whereby the workings of government, on behalf
of citizens, can be revealed to them).

14. Under international human rights law, the right to privacy and the RTI are equally weighted (see Banisar 2011).

15. Though European decisions have favored disclosure over privacy in decisions about public figures' financial information, in a very important case, the European Court of Justice favored privacy over disclosure in the context of Internet search engine results and the "right to be forgotten." See European Commission, Factsheet on the "Right to be Forgotten" ruling (C-131/12), http://ec.europa.eu/justice/data-protection/files/factsheets/factsheet_data_protection_en.pdf.

16. The full text of the statement of principles is available at http://www.opensociety foundations.org/fact-sheets/tshwane-principles-national-security-and-right-information -overview-15-points.

17. Case cited in Banisar (2011, 16).

18. The factors to consider in determining whether an oversight body is sufficiently independent and can function effectively to perform oversight duties are discussed in chapter 3, box 3.6.

19. Daniel Kahneman's book *Thinking Fast and Slow* provides an excellent overview of some of the research on cognitive bias and its effects on decision making (see Kahneman 2011). Though there is anecdotal evidence of the effects of cognitive bias on decision making on the application of RTI exemption provisions, this area has not been studied systematically.

20. FOIAnet (2013, 16); see also case studies on Albania, Moldova, and Romania in Trapnell (2014).

References

Baitarian, Lori. 2015. "Sudan Passes Freedom of Information Law but Journalists Remain Wary." Committee to Protect Journalists. https://cpj.org/blog/2015/02/sudan-passes -freedom-of-information-law-but-journa.php.

Banisar, David. 2011. *The Right to Information and Privacy: Balancing Rights and Managing Conflicts*. Washington, DC: World Bank. https://www.ip-rs.si/fileadmin/user_upload /Pdf/Publikacije_ostalih_pooblascencev/Right_to_Information_and_Privacy__banisar .pdf.

Berliner, Daniel. 2012. "Institutionalizing Transparency: The Global Spread of Freedom of Information Law and Practice." Unpublished PhD dissertation, University of Washington. https://digital.lib.washington.edu/researchworks/handle/1773/21770.

Calland, Richard. 2003. "Turning Right to Information Law into a Living Reality: Access to Information and the Imperative of Effective Implementation." Open Democracy Advice Centre, Cape Town. http://www.humanrightsinitiative.org/programs/ai/rti /international/laws_papers/southafrica/Calland%20-%20Turning%20FOI%20law%20 into%20living%20reality%20-%20Jan-03.pdf.

Carothers, Thomas, and Saskia Brechenmacher. 2014. *Accountability, Transparency, Participation, and Inclusion: A New Development Consensus?* Washington, DC: Carnegie Endowment for International Peace. http://carnegieendowment.org/files /new_development_consensus.pdf.

Centre for Law and Democracy. 2015. "Submission to the Office of the Special Rapporteur on the Protection and Promotion of the Right to Freedom of Opinion and Expression on Encryption and Anonymity in Digital Communications." Centre for Law and Democracy, Halifax.

Centre for Law and Democracy and Africa Freedom of Information Centre. 2014. *Right to Information Training Manual for African Public Officials*. Centre for Law and Democracy, Halifax.

Darbishire, Helen. 2010. "Proactive Transparency: The Future of the Right to Information? A Review of Standards, Challenges, and Opportunities." Working Paper, World Bank, Washington, DC. http://siteresources.worldbank.org/WBI/Resources /213798-1259011531325/6598384-1268250334206/Darbishire_Proactive _Transparency.pdf.

Dokeniya, Anupama. 2013. "The Right to Information as a Tool for Community Empowerment." *World Bank Legal Review* 5: 599–614.

———. 2014a. "Implementing Right to Information: A Case Study of Uganda." In *Right to Information: Case Studies on Implementation*, edited by Stephanie E. Trapnell, 275–316. Right to Information Series. Washington, DC: World Bank. http:// siteresources.worldbank.org/PUBLICSECTORANDGOVERNANCE/Resources /285741-1343934891414/8787489-1344020463266/8788935-1399321576201 /RTI_Case_Studies_Implementation_WEBfinal.pdf.

———. 2014b. "The Right to Information as a Tool for Community Empowerment." In *The World Bank Legal Review, Volume 5: Fostering Development through Opportunity, Inclusion, and Equity*, edited by Hassan Cisse, N. R. Madhava Menon, Marie-Claire Cordonier Segger, and Vincent O. Nmehielle, 599–614. Washington, DC: World Bank. https://openknowledge.worldbank.org/bitstream/handle/10986/16240/82558 .pdf?sequence=1.

Florini, Ann. 1999. "Does the Invisible Hand Need a Transparent Glove? The Politics of Transparency." Paper prepared for the Annual World Bank Conference on Development Economics, Washington, DC, April 28–30. http://siteresources.worldbank.org/DEC /Resources/84797-1251813753820/6415739-1251814010799/florini.pdf.

FOIAnet. 2013. "Global Right to Information Update: An Analysis by Region." Freedom of Information Advocates Network. http://foiadvocates.net/?avada_portfolio=global -right-to-information-update-an-analysis-by-region.

Greenwald, Glenn. 2013. "NSA Collecting Phone Records of Millions of Verizon Customers Daily." *The Guardian*, June 6.

Holsen, Sarah, and Martial Pasquier. 2012. "Insight on Oversight: The Role of Information Commissioners in the Implementation of Access to Information Policies." *Journal of Information Policy* 2: 214–41.

Kahneman, Daniel. 2011. *Thinking Fast and Slow*. New York: Farrar, Straus and Giroux.

Levy, Brian. 2014. *Working with the Grain: Integrating Governance and Growth in Development Strategies*. Oxford: Oxford University Press.

McClean, Thomas. 2011. "Shackling Leviathan: A Comparative Historical Study of Institutions and the Adoption of Freedom of Information." Unpublished dissertation, London School of Economics.

Mendel, Toby. 2009. *Freedom of Information in Latin America: A Comparative Legal Survey*. New York: UNESCO.

———. 2014. *Recent Spread of RTI Legislation*. Right to Information Paper Series. Washington DC: World Bank.

———. 2015. *Designing Right to Information Laws for Effective Implementation*. Right to Information Series. Washington, DC: World Bank.

Michener, Greg. 2011. *Towards an Agenda-Setting Theory of Freedom of Information: The Case of Latin America*. 1st Global Conference on Transparency Research, Rutgers University, Newark, New Jersey, May 19–20. https://spaa.newark.rutgers.edu/sites /default/files/files/Transparency_Research_Conference/Papers/Michener_Greg _Paper_one.pdf

OECD. 2015. *Regulatory Policy in Perspective: A Reader's Companion to the OECD Regulatory Policy Outlook 2015*. Paris: OECD Publishing.

Open Government Partnership. 2015. "How It Works: Eligibility Criteria." http://www .opengovpartnership.org/how-it-works/eligibility-criteria.

Open Society Justice Initiative. 2006. *Transparency and Silence: A Survey of Access to Information Laws and Practices in 14 Countries*. New York: Open Society Institute. http://www.opensocietyfoundations.org/sites/default/files/transparency_20060928 .pdf.

———. 2013. *The Global Principles on National Security and the Right to Information* ["The Tschwane Principles"]. New York: Open Society Institute.

Peixoto, Tiago. 2013. "Does Transparency Lead to Trust? Some Evidence on the Subject." *DemocracySpot*, June 19. http://democracyspot.net/2013/06/19/does-transparency -lead-to-trust-some-evidence-on-the-subject.

Roberts, Alasdair. 2006. *Blacked Out: Government Secrecy in the Information Age*. Cambridge: Cambridge University Press.

Solove, Daniel J., and Paul Schwartz. 2008. *Information Privacy Law*. 3rd ed. New York: Aspen Publishers.

Trapnell, Stephanie E., ed. 2014. *Right to Information: Case Studies on Implementation*. Right to Information Series. Washington, DC: World Bank. http://www-wds.worldbank .org/external/default/WDSContentServer/WDSP/IB/2015/08/04/090224b08304 cac4/1_0/Rendered/PDF/Right0to0infor0es0on0implementation.pdf.

United Nations OHCHR (Office of the High Commissioner for Human Rights). 1998. "Report of the Special Rapporteur on the Promotion and Protection of the Right to Freedom of Opinion and Expression." Symbol E/CN.4/1998/CN.4/1998/40. United Nations, New York.

———. 2014. "The Right to Privacy in the Digital Age." United Nations, New York. http:// www.ohchr.org/EN/HRBodies/HRC/RegularSessions/Session27/Documents/A.HRC .27.37_en.pdf.

World Bank. 2004. *World Development Report 2004: Making Services Work for Poor People*. Washington, DC: World Bank.

Further Reading

Berliner, Daniel. 2014. "The Political Origins of Transparency." *Journal of Politics* 76 (2): 479–91.

Carter, Megan, and Andrew Bouris. 2006. *Freedom of Information: Balancing the Public Interest*. 2nd ed. London: Constitution Unit, School of Public Policy, University College London. https://www.ucl.ac.uk/spp/publications/unit-publications/134.pdf.

Dokeniya, Anupama. 2013. *Implementing Right to Information: Lessons from Experience*. Washington, DC: World Bank. http://siteresources.worldbank.org /PUBLICSECTORANDGOVERNANCE/Resources/285741-1343934891414 /8787489-1344020463266/RTI-IPP-Web-Final.pdf.

Dror, Yebezkel. 1999. "Transparency and Openness of Quality Democracy." In *Openness and Transparency in Governance: Challenges and Opportunities*, edited by Michael Kelly, 25–43. Maastricht: NISPAcee Forum.

Fung, Archon. 2008. *Full Disclosure: The Perils and Promise of Transparency*. New York: Cambridge University Press.

Heald, David. 2006. "Varieties of Transparency." In *Transparency: The Key to Better Governance?* edited by Christopher Hood and David Heald. New York: Oxford University Press/British Academy.

Sharma, Prashant. 2014. *Democracy and Transparency in the Indian State: The Making of the Right to Information Act*. Routledge/Edinburgh South Asian Studies Series. New York: Routledge.

CHAPTER 3

Considering the Domains of RTI Implementation

Section 1: Enabling Conditions

Enabling conditions for right to information (RTI) implementation need to be in place both within and outside the public sector, and such conditions are far broader than just RTI laws. They include a well-designed legal framework, as well as a functioning civil society with the capacity to engage with government and to advocate for reform. Also included are political stability[1] and ongoing policy prioritization from executive or legislative leadership that signals the importance of RTI policies within government agencies.

Wider Legal Framework

The implementation of RTI is critically influenced by the quality of the laws that establish the entitlement to information. As discussed in chapter 2, weaknesses in the RTI law can, in fact, lead to various implementation problems.

The laws establishing the enabling legal environment for participation and enforcement are also fundamentally important to the successful functioning of an RTI system. This wider legal framework provides scope for advocacy by civil society organizations (CSOs) and the private sector, by creating the foundation for participation and influence, which are important factors contributing to the sustainability of the RTI. Box 3.1 provides a list of laws that provide the basis for a strong enabling environment.

Weak enabling environments can inhibit effective implementation of even well-designed RTI laws, whereas stronger enabling environments may compensate for weak RTI laws. Table 3.1 highlights the CIVICUS Enabling Environment Index (EEI) country scores on a variety of measures associated with rights and freedoms of civil society.[2] Higher scores on associational rights appear to have only a weak relationship with better functioning RTI laws (e.g., India, Mexico, the United Kingdom, and the United States), except where the law itself falls below 85 out of 150 (e.g., Albania, Romania, Uganda), as shown in the comparison with the Global RTI Rating score of laws. In these latter cases, the

Box 3.1 Laws Making Up the Enabling Legal Environment

Political rights and freedoms

- Political stability and absence of violence
- Political participation
- Political culture
- Human rights

Associational rights

- Freedom of assembly and association

Rule of law

- Strength of legal framework and enforceability
- Electoral process and pluralism
- Independence of the judiciary

NGO legal context

- Legal conditions allowing NGOs to operate

Media freedoms

- Freedom of speech
- Media freedom
- Freedom on the Internet

Source: CIVICUS Enabling Environment Index 2013, http://civicus.org/eei/.

Table 3.1 Scores on Enabling Legal Environment

Country	CIVICUS political rights and freedoms	CIVICUS associational rights	CIVICUS rule of law	CIVICUS personal rights	CIVICUS NGO legal context	CIVICUS media freedoms	Average CIVICUS score	Comparison with Global RTI Rating law score (0–150)
Albania	0.58	0.94	0.44	0.78	0.52	0.60	0.64	69
India	0.43	0.75	0.56	0.36	—	0.55	0.53	130
Jordan	0.35	0.22	0.42	0.33	—	0.37	0.34	55
Mexico	0.43	0.89	0.47	0.29	—	0.53	0.52	119
Moldova	0.49	0.33	0.50	0.60	0.47	0.66	0.51	110
Peru	0.57	0.64	0.60	0.72	—	0.55	0.62	95
Romania	0.62	0.75	0.62	0.61	0.57	0.67	0.64	83
South Africa	0.60	0.94	0.70	0.41	0.62	0.70	0.66	111
Thailand	0.36	0.58	0.56	0.26	—	0.31	0.41	76
Uganda	0.39	0.28	0.46	0.46	0.32	0.39	0.38	98
United Kingdom	0.83	1.00	0.85	0.82	—	0.89	0.88	99
United States	0.71	1.00	0.82	0.78	—	0.91	0.84	89

Source: CIVICUS Enabling Environment Index 2013, http://civicus.org/eei/. For methodology of the Global RTI Ratings, see http://www.rti-rating .org/methodology.
Note: NGO = nongovernmental organization; RTI = right to information; — = data not available.

nongovernmental organization (NGO) legal context scores are also much lower, implying that rights and freedoms for organizations may provide an additional boost in support of RTI implementation.

Although enabling rights and freedoms may not have to be in place before the establishment of the RTI, they should be considered complementary and equally important to effective implementation and therefore, if weak, should be strengthened throughout the implementation of an RTI law.

Advocacy Efforts

The efforts of CSOs, media groups and journalists, and academics are instrumental in the formation and implementation of RTI laws. In fact, lack of civil society involvement in the passage of the RTI law can correlate with lack of ownership of the law by citizens and very slow implementation progress due to a lack of demand (Lipcean and Stefan 2014; Meknassi 2014; Nicro, Vornpien, and Chancharoen 2014; Trapnell and Lemieux 2014; Trebicka and Shella 2014).[3] This is true even in countries with more active civil societies. In some cases, CSOs may be well positioned to conduct compliance testing on the rates and quality of response from government, which can be compared to self-reported data from administrative systems to provide a more accurate understanding of agency performance.

CSOs are comparatively less involved in RTI implementation where there is a lack of civic space for this kind of engagement, such as in environments where NGO communities are heavily regulated or political rights are restricted, acting as a deterrent to the establishment and activities of CSOs. Similarly, in contexts where political participation is restricted or when the public has little confidence in the capabilities of NGOs, advocacy efforts can be hampered. Even in challenging environments, however, organizations in many countries find ways to engage in advocacy efforts, including lobbying, strategic litigation, and monitoring of implementation (see table 3.2).

Table 3.2 Most Common Civil Society Advocacy Efforts on RTI Issues

Country	Involved in passage of law	Lobbying for/against amendments	Strategic litigation	Monitoring of implementation
Albania	–	+	–	–
India	+	+	+	+
Jordan	–	+	+	+
Mexico	+	+	+	+
Moldova	–	+	+	–
Peru	+	+	+	+
Romania	+	+	+	+
South Africa	+	+	+	+
Thailand	–	+	–	–
Uganda	+	+	–	+
United Kingdom	+	+	+	+
United States	+	+	+	+
	8/12	12/12	9/12	9/12

Source: Trapnell and Lemieux 2014 and CIVICUS Enabling Environment Index 2013, http://civicus.org/eei/.
Note: RTI = right to information.

Policy Prioritization

Policy prioritization is the extent to which high-level officials within government signal their support for RTI. Such signaling events consequently impact upon the strength of the strategic and operational leadership of senior public officials engaged in the management of the public sector. It encompasses both political will and sustained support for reform as they manifest in practical, tangible support for the implementation of RTI laws. Indeed, political support is a major driver of sustainable and effective implementation (Dokeniya 2013; Trapnell and Lemieux 2014).[4]

Berliner and Erlich present evidence suggesting that passage and reform of RTI laws has been shown in some cases to be driven by political competition, whereby politicians in power seek to ensure future access to government information by initiating legal reforms, as insurance against being shut out of power should they lose their seats in government (Berliner and Erlich 2015). Policy prioritization takes support for reform one step further; it is about both reform and implementation sustainability. Without prioritization of RTI implementation, particularly at the beginning of the implementation process, the sustainability of reform efforts is limited. Public expressions of support for RTI by politicians and ministers are common; however, in robust RTI systems, there is not only public pronouncement of support for RTI implementation, there is also clear evidence of sustained, well-funded initiatives supported by high-level political figures, such as presidents and members of parliament (Alexander 2014; Mizrahi and Mendiburu 2014; Trapnell 2014).[5] In these kinds of robust systems, CSOs and media are predominantly active and *influential* in either advocacy or collaborative activities.

Many reasons may account for lack of political support for the RTI, leading to ineffective or absent initiatives that fail to prioritize RTI implementation. Instability and conflict have hindered implementation and, by extension, limited the prioritization of RTI within the public sector, in some former Soviet Bloc states and most recently in the Republic of Yemen (Lipcean and Stefan 2014, 163; Trebicka and Shella 2014, 11). The push for accession into the European Union initially drove implementation in some countries, helped in particular by the publication of league tables that assessed implementation efforts, but political interest has subsequently tapered off (Ionita and Stefan 2014, 244, 250). The case in South Africa is similar, where post-apartheid reforms led to the adoption of an RTI law but little effort toward implementation (Moses 2014, 458). Politicians and bureaucrats in other countries view RTI as a tool for administrative investigations and ousting officials from government, and thus in these countries there is little political support (Nicro, Vornpien, and Chancharoen 2014, 482, 518).

RTI policy prioritization does not follow a singular model across countries. Instead, it is a rather fluid feature of RTI implementation, in that it depends on country context, both legal and political, and timing. Nevertheless, it should be considered a central feature in the sustainability of RTI implementation.

Section 2: Demand for Information

Demand for information is a critical factor in the effectiveness of RTI systems, because underutilized systems tend to be underdeveloped and exhibit poor performance. Knowledge, motivation, and accessibility are constraints on access to information. The accessibility of RTI systems is significantly influenced by the extent of public awareness about information rights and RTI processes. In turn, knowledge of RTI processes is enhanced through repeated interactions with agencies concerning information disclosure.

The most common, and most sophisticated, users of RTI are media, CSOs, academics, and the private sector. Many of these groups utilize RTI in the interest of research, policy making, and investigative reporting. But information on the types of individuals or organizations requesting information is limited by the data collected by governments. In 2013, 95 percent of the requesters in Brazil were individuals, and nearly 5 percent were businesses. In Mexico, 68 percent of requesters were individuals, 15 percent were businesses, 8 percent were other government agencies, 5 percent were media, and 4 percent were CSOs (Worker with Excell 2014). Few data are available on the use of RTI by marginalized groups, who are most likely to use RTI to engender change that affects the lives of ordinary citizens, including improvement of education, health services, access to water, infrastructure, and even battling petty corruption at the municipal level as in the example in box 3.2.

Box 3.2 Demand for Information by Local Activists and Organizations in Uganda

Construction (2014): A Ugandan activist filed an information request for records pertaining to the construction of Kashenyi Health Centre II with Bushenyi-Ishaka Town Council. His request was prompted by unconfirmed information that government had allegedly paid for 210 iron sheets to roof a structure at the Health Centre, yet physical count showed only 56 iron sheets. On receipt of the information request, the town clerk invited him for a discussion and unsuccessfully attempted to bribe him with U Sh 500,000 (US$200) to give up his request for records. Once this action was reported to the Bushenyi District Local Government, leaders led by the chairperson, Mr. Willis Bashasha, demanded urgent action on the misuse of public funds by Ishaka-Bushenyi Town Council.

Health supplies (2014): In Masaka District, central Uganda, communities had suffered years of frustration about the lack of medicines for malaria, the main cause of sickness and death among Ugandan women and children. A shortage of malaria medicine at health facilities was a common problem in the district. One of the participants at the workshop filed a FOIA request for information regarding the number of times Mpugwe Health Centre had received medicines for malaria and the number of doses in each delivery. It was found that despite the chronic absence of medicine, the Health Centre had regularly

box continues next page

Box 3.2 Demand for Information by Local Activists and Organizations in Uganda *(continued)*

received supplies. The activist demanded that this information should be displayed at the Health Centre's public notice board, following which there was no reported shortage of medicine for several weeks.

Implementing rules (2011): On February 21, 2011, the Africa Freedom of Information Centre (AFIC) made an information request to the rt. hon. prime minister of Uganda requesting information regarding how each minister was complying with Section 43 of the Access to Information Act in respect to annual reports to parliament. In her letter to AFIC dated April 15, 2011, the minister of information and national guidance acting on the prime minister's directive regretted the failure to comply with reporting and explained that lack of access to information regulations under Section 47 of the Access to Information Act was the reason for ministers' lack of compliance with annual reporting. She promised that regulations would be issued within two months. Indeed, a week later, April 21, 2011, Access to Information Regulations 2011 No. 17 were gazetted.

Source: Africa Freedom of Information Centre, 2014, http://www.africafoicentre.org.
Note: FOIA = Freedom of Information Act.

An understanding of rights, as well as having accessibility to processes, matters for marginalized groups in very practical ways. Language differences, low literacy levels, unfamiliarity with bureaucratic procedures, and lack of Internet access are all major factors that prevent large numbers of people from accessing information request processes. Public awareness of RTI influences not only the ability of requesters to access information, but also their understanding of the information rights accorded to them. Knowledge of what can be requested, and how information can assist with certain goals (which motivates request making) is also part of this equation. The success of information requests is based upon the technical knowledge needed to formulate requests, as well as the broader knowledge of the kinds of information that can, and should, be requested. As a result, some studies have expressed concern that requesters make up a potentially narrow social base of specialist information requesters centered in urban areas (Fox and Haight 2011, 156). Request data collected by governments between 2011 and 2013 indicate that the ratio of requests to population is less than 1 percent across a sample of eight countries (Worker with Excell 2014). One implication is that the group of requesters that make up the bulk of requests may constitute an extremely small proportion of the population. Questions of representativeness and inclusion abound, potentially compromising the inclusiveness of access to information initiatives. However, it is important to consider that RTI systems function in a manner analogous to court systems that support accountability and fair societies but are not expected to be used by all people all the time (see table 3.3).

Lack of access based on gender, race, and class is also a fundamental issue compromising the inclusiveness of RTI systems, though only weakly addressed in the country cases underpinning our framework for effective RTI

Table 3.3 Legal Obligations for Government Bodies Regarding RTI Accessibility

Country	Assistance in formulating and clarifying requests	Assistance for special needs requesters	No cost or fee waivers available[a]
Max score	2	2	
Albania	0	0	Neither
India	2	2	Fee waivers
Jordan	0	0	No cost
Mexico	2	2	No cost
Moldova	2	0	No cost
Peru	2	0	No cost
Romania	1	0	No cost
South Africa	2	2	Fee waivers
Thailand	0	0	Fee waivers
Uganda	2	2	Neither
United Kingdom	2	2	Neither
United States	1	2	Neither
Average	1.3 out of 2	1 out of 2	

Source: Access Info Europe and the Centre for Law and Democracy's Global Right to Information (RTI) Rating, 2014, http://www.rti-rating.org/country-data.
a. Does not include appeals.

implementation (Trapnell 2014). In a separate study from Liberia on gender and RTI, perceptions of mixed-gender groups confirmed that women access information much less often than men, a finding that was also confirmed through observations of RTI units within government agencies. Aggregate data from interviews demonstrate that the barriers preventing women from exercising their RTI include illiteracy, fear of asking, and not knowing how to ask or where to go to find or request information. Responsibilities for household and child care, as well as mobility and distance to government agencies, are also cited as significant barriers (Carter Center 2014b, 25–28). These findings suggest that further study of the relationship between RTI systems and different social and ethnic groups is essential to making the RTI equally, and fairly, accessible to all. Box 3.3 provides examples from case studies of the obstacles to accessing information through RTI.

Information requests are the primary channels for individuals to communicate their specific demands for information to government bodies. There is a learning curve associated with obtaining satisfactory responses to information requests, as requesters must know *how* and *what* to request from government bodies. In terms of providing access to information, information intermediaries such as CSOs and media play a critical role in their analysis and dissemination of information, but they also serve as filters through their own sets of lenses. Public outreach and promotional measures are an overlooked aspect of government responsibility, even when mandated by law. It is important to make requesters aware of their rights and to provide assistance in the information request processes if participation in the information access regime is to be considered a success (see table 3.4).

Box 3.3 Obstacles to Accessing Information through RTI

Requesters may face a variety of obstacles to accessibility besides knowledge of procedures, which can be compounded by language and technical difficulties:

- Petty corruption is cited as a concern in Albania and Uganda, where soft money is used not to expedite requests, but rather to ensure that requests are accepted, with no guarantee of a quality response.
- Personal connections are important again in Albania, but also in Jordan, where informality in request processing is a result of the low number of requests, further exacerbating the problem.
- In Jordan, there is simply no form available to request information in most ministries, even though it is mandated by law. In addition, a reason for use of the information must be provided by requesters to obtain a response.
- Language difficulties are a prevailing factor in the low demand for information in South Africa, because requesters struggle with not only formulating a request, but also understanding the rules for submitting requests.
- Despite the high volume of requests in India, with remarkable successes in securing accountability in some areas, citizens still face a lack of information on the filing process, and they are regularly unable to find contact information for submission at district and local government levels.

Source: Compilation based on Trapnell 2014.

Table 3.4 Barriers to the Appeals Process

Country	Lack of internal appeals process (e.g., public body)	Lack of external appeals authority (e.g., information commissioner)	Lack of accommodation in judicial process for nonexpert filers
Albania	−	+	+
India	−	−	+
Jordan	+	−	+
Mexico	−	−	+
Moldova	−	+	+
Peru	−	+	+
Romania	−	+	+
South Africa	−	+	+
Thailand	+	−	−
Uganda	−	+	+
United Kingdom	−	−	+
United States	−	+	+
	2/12	7/12	11/12

Source: Trapnell and Lemieux 2014.

Barriers to appeals, as a further step in the information disclosure chain, also diminish demand for information (see box 3.4). The first level of appeal is usually at the same organization that receives the initial request. In many contexts, the second level of appeal is with the judicial system and offers little assistance to users, discouraging them from pursuing requests further. Requests from the general population[6] face considerable obstacles to the judicial appeals process, for reasons having to do with a lack of expertise, high costs, and problematic judicial authority. Many countries provide for a second-level appeal at an independent, nonjudicial authority, such as an information commission or council. Appeals to these kinds of authorities do not require substantial fees or expertise, the processes are simplified for maximum accessibility, and decisions are often binding.

Innovative approaches to making information more accessible to marginalized communities combine functions such as assistance to requesters, communication about the content of a request, clarification or negotiation of what is an acceptable and meaningful response, and complaints processes.[7] In effective RTI regimes, such services typically are located strategically near populations of potential information requesters. The Oportunidades program in Mexico has a specific citizen attention window through which most of the information requests and complaints are managed (Fox and Haight 2011, 157; Mizrahi and Mendiburu 2014, 121). It is important to note that both requests and complaints are addressed through this unit, and citizens engage and discuss with government the kinds of information that they are seeking.

The accessibility of RTI processes and procedures is of paramount importance to the demand for information and the extent of inclusiveness of RTI systems. Very little information has been systematically collected on the reach

---

Box 3.4 Barriers to the RTI Judicial Process in Several Countries

Many countries face obstacles when dealing with the RTI appeals process, for reasons having to do with expertise, costs, and a problematic judicial authority.

- In Peru, a legal suit is filed through the constitutional action of *habeas data*, which must be maintained over time, and even then, decisions may not be applied as general rules that set precedents.
- Appeals in the South African courts are complex and expensive, deterring most requesters from pursuing information disclosure through this option.
- Judicial review is such a complex deterrent in Albania that few appeals have ever been filed.
- The High Court in Jordan often refuses to hear RTI cases, and it is not clear if decisions by the lower appeals authority are binding on agencies.
- The judiciary in Uganda is considered to be prone to political influence and lacks the technical capacity to address RTI issues.

Source: Trapnell 2014.
Note: RTI = right to information.

---

of RTI systems with regard to marginalized communities. Realization of the full potential of RTI systems to meaningfully affect the lives of citizens relies upon opportunities for participation that extend to all citizens, regardless of gender, race, class, or location. Moreover, when political support wanes or oversight capacity deteriorates, the impetus to continue disclosing information is weakened. Demand can serve as a driving force for reform in these circumstances, in addition to helping to ensure sustainability and collaboration.

Section 3: Institutional Capacity

Institutional capacity refers to both the specialist and nonspecialist functions of bureaucracies, including records management, strategic planning, personnel management, and monitoring progress toward institutional goals that are necessary for effective operation of RTI systems. Poor operational performance in RTI is often the result of a combination of factors: resource-constrained environments and a lack of internal commitment, combined with a lack of training and employment incentives, resulting in poor performance. Improvements in institutional capacity primarily take root when they involve broad sets of agents engaged together in designing and implementing locally; that is, lasting change is not always driven from the top down (Andrews, Pritchett, and Woolcock 2012). In this chapter, we highlight the higher-level, broad features of institutional capacity that our research suggests must drive effective implementation of RTI laws.

Updated, Formal Practices

Internal rules and administrative regulations are important for incorporating legal obligations into agency processes and activities. These rules lay the groundwork for institutionalization of RTI practices. Formalization here refers to the extent to which agencies have institutionalized their legal obligations into formal practices, procedures, and institutional arrangements that support the basic functions in an RTI system at the agency level.

No RTI system will function adequately without clear, formalized procedures that remove opportunities for discretionary decision making that can lead to abuse, set appropriate incentives for civil servants and managers to support its implementation, and encourage leadership across levels of government that signals commitment to the regular practice of information disclosure. These formalized practices are particularly important for request processing, records management, and proactive disclosure, because these areas form the backbone of an RTI system.

Request processing, records management, and proactive disclosure are three fundamental practices of RTI systems, and their formalization merits discussion within this general framework for implementation. Organizational policies and administrative decisions that structure these three practices within organizations are addressed in chapter 4.

Request Processing

Informal requests for information have always been prevalent among some user groups, such as journalists and CSOs, because they need expedited means of obtaining information. This is often necessary in time-sensitive cases that pertain to public interest and the public good. There is no reason that informal requests of this nature should pose a problem for formalized information disclosure. However, some countries struggle with overcoming a tradition of informal networks in the information request process, or petty corruption in frontline offices, that serves to exclude individuals and groups outside of the ruling elite and reinforce established power dynamics (Dokeniya 2014, 300; Meknassi 2014, 388; Trebicka and Shella 2014, 34).

Formalization of the information request process is important as a means of providing access beyond a specialist group of users. Informality in the requesting process precludes reliable tracking of activities, because requests are not registered, departments holding information may not be consulted, and the basis for appeals is preempted. Even though formal requesting procedures may lengthen the process for obtaining information, they are essential for institutionalizing processes and embedding information disclosure in public authorities, rather than relying upon the decisions of a few individuals. At the same time, care must be taken not to overly bureaucratize the process of information requests.

Records Management

The successful implementation of RTI laws is tightly coupled with governments' ability to create and maintain—and ultimately make available—information about their actions and decisions. This information is usually found in the form of "records," which, according to the international records management standard (ISO 15489), are "information created, received, and maintained as evidence and information by an organization or person, in pursuance of legal obligations or in the transaction of business" (ISO 2001, 3).[8] As Laura Millar observes, "When citizens seek answers using 'access to information' legislation, they are not expecting a public servant to provide that information verbally" (Millar 2003, 1). This is because records, being created in the usual and ordinary course of business as government decisions and actions are taken, are likely to provide objective evidence of those decisions and actions, whereas a verbal account of the same decisions and actions may be subject to the fallibility of human memory or to other distortions of the facts.

Trustworthy records and information do not come about by themselves, however. Rather, their existence and subsequent availability are dependent upon good records management practices, that is, upon "the efficient and systematic control of the creation, receipt, maintenance, use and disposition of records, including processes for capturing and maintaining evidence of and information about business activities and transactions in the form of records."[9] Records management authorities provide much-needed guidance to agencies on the proper destruction of records, electronic records management, archiving procedures, use of resources, and performance monitoring. In Mexico, the United Kingdom, and the United States, records management authorities (see table 3.5) collaborate with RTI oversight bodies to harmonize record-keeping policies across the public sector (Alexander 2014; Mizrahi and Mendiburu 2014). In these countries, there are ongoing efforts to standardize record-keeping practices for the benefit of RTI. However, as indicated in table 3.3, such collaboration is not a common practice.

Unfortunately, for many governments, records management is a low priority, which has resulted in informality in record creation and keeping (Millar 2003, 2).[10] This informality means that standards are not maintained. In fact, poor records management practices produce poor records. This practice results not only in delays in responding to information requests, but also in lower-quality and even unreliable information being distributed about government activities (Lemieux 2016). It also prevents effective collection of data on government functioning, posing a significant obstacle to the success of proactive disclosure of information (Lemieux, Petrov, and Burks 2014).

Records management is becoming even more challenging for governments with the introduction of new information and communication technologies (ICTs). These technologies have transformed the way in which people communicate with one another and how such communications are recorded and preserved. A good example of this transformation is the increasing use of e-mail and social media communications, now used quite widely to transact government

Table 3.5 Records Management Oversight Arrangements

Country	Records management (RM) oversight authority	Collaboration between RM and RTI monitoring bodies
Albania	National Archives	–
India	Department of Administrative Reforms and Public Grievances	–
Jordan	Department of the National Library	–
Mexico	National Archives	+
Moldova	Secretariat Administrative Services	–
Peru	General Archive of the Nation	–
Romania	National Archives	–
South Africa	National Archives and Records Service	–
Thailand	National Archives	–
Uganda	Department of Records Information Management in the Ministry of Public Service (records management), Ministry of Information and National Guidance (retrieval and dissemination)	–
United Kingdom	National Archives	+
United States	National Archives and Records Administration	+
	12/12	3/12

Source: Trapnell and Lemieux 2014.
Note: RTI = right to information.

business in many countries. Uncertainty prevails in some countries about whether these new forms of recorded communication are records, and, if so, how they should be treated under public records and RTI laws. In the United States, there has been extensive litigation focused on clarifying how e-mails and other digital forms of communication should be treated under the U.S. Federal Records and the Freedom of Information Acts.[11] In Canada, the province of British Columbia's information and privacy commissioner has investigated government practices around the handling of digital forms of communication, finding evidence of systemic deliberate deletion of e-mails to avoid being responsive to requests for information, while also holding that it is clear that such recorded communications are records for purposes of RTI.

Equally unclear in some contexts is the question of whether requests for information under RTI laws can be made using new digital forms of communication. In a recent international survey, information commissioners were asked whether requests made using social media would be valid in their countries. Thirty-five percent felt that generally such requests would be valid, and 30 percent said they could never be valid. Many commissioners had not yet had to deal with an appeal regarding refusal of such a request, which perhaps explains why 25 percent said they did not know if they were valid or not (Centre for Freedom of Information 2014). Given that many public authorities use e-mail and social media to communicate, there is a need for greater clarity on how to treat these new forms of recorded information in relation to public records and RTI laws and regulation.

Though weak records management presents a challenge to effective implementation of RTI laws, it is not an insurmountable one. There is broad international consensus on the elements that need to be in place to support effective record keeping, which makes it much easier for countries to chart a path to strengthening their records management systems. Appendix E provides a summary of several relevant international records management standards. In addition, NGOs have produced resources that can be used to guide improvements to records management systems (see, for example, Open Government Partnership 2015). That said, addressing records management weaknesses across the board can strain resources, and, like many other types of information systems, efforts to introduce electronic records management systems have a high risk of failure. This has led to reluctance on the part of some officials to make necessary improvements to records management to support implementation of RTI laws. In light of past experience with records management initiatives, targeted, incremental approaches may work best.

Proactive Disclosure

One of the most cited practices for lowering the administrative burden and financial costs of request processing is proactive disclosure. Proactive disclosure of information in RTI laws refers to the release of information to the public without an initial request. This includes information in bulk form (i.e., a dataset) which is released via an online public portal, as is typical of open data initiatives (see box 3.5). Most RTI laws contain proactive disclosure provisions. In addition,

Box 3.5 Open Data Defined

The concept of open data is relatively new. It originated with the belief that the enormous amount of information routinely collected by government entities should be available to all citizens. In the late 2000s, governments and entities began to allow a greater number of users access to these resources. The first government policies on open data appeared in 2009. Today more than 250 governments at national, subnational, and city levels and almost 50 developed and developing countries, and entities such as the World Bank and United Nations, have launched open data initiatives—and more are launched every year.

Data are considered to be "open" if anyone can freely use, reuse, and redistribute them, for any purpose, without restrictions. Although a large amount of data is published on government websites, the majority of published data is intended only to be read as stand-alone documents, not reused for other purposes. To be considered "open," the data must be reusable, meaning they can be downloaded in open formats and read by software, and users have a legal right to reuse the data.

Source: World Bank, "Open Data Essentials," http://opendatatoolkit.worldbank.org/en/essentials.html.

many other laws and regulations (such as laws and regulations relating to procurement) have requirements for proactive disclosure.

The advantage of proactive disclosure is that people do not have to submit a formal request or wait on a decision—they can access the information immediately. On the other hand, the type and scope of proactively disclosed information may not meet the needs of all people, the quality of the information can often be poor, and, unless the requirement to release it is ensconced in law, oversight may be difficult and public agencies may discontinue disclosure. The assessment of proactive disclosure is also a difficult task, because there are no agreed standards as to the amount, regularity, or content of information that should be disclosed. There are currently only general recommendations about regular postings and serious concerns over the quality, relevance, and comprehensibility of information being disclosed to citizens. We discuss these issues further in chapter 4.

Proactively disclosed information has many similarities with open data, even though the roots of open data are not in RTI. Open data originated with the belief that the enormous amount of information routinely collected by government entities should be available to all citizens (World Bank 2015). The first government policies on open data appeared in 2009 in the United Kingdom and the United States (World Bank 2015). A global movement to make government "open by default" gained support in 2013 when the G-8 leaders signed an Open Data Charter that promised to make public sector data openly available, without charge and in reuseable formats (World Wide Web Foundation 2015). In 2014, the G-20 largest industrial economies followed up by pledging to advance open data as a tool against corruption (World Wide Web Foundation 2015). Many governments now have open data initiatives.

Although proactive disclosure and open data have different origins and communities of support, recently there has been greater recognition of the advantages of creating closer ties and greater collaboration on RTI and open data agendas (see, for example, Fumega 2015). New research suggests that RTI laws provide support to open data initiatives in important ways: (1) by including proactive disclosure provisions in laws that establish a legal duty to disclose; (2) by providing a means for citizens, firms, and others to request information that has not been proactively disclosed but that is relevant to their interests; (3) by providing guidance on exemptions to disclosure that clarifies what can be disclosed proactively; and (4) by establishing institutional structures that support disclosure, such as information commissioners, oversight mechanisms, and complaints mechanisms (Cambridge Economic Associates and PDG South Africa 2014).

Proactive disclosure provisions generally focus on releasing datasets about government operations, as well as the data that the government collects and uses to make policy decisions. Categories of relevant information include administrative data, expenditures and accounts, policy reports, internal procedures and functions, human resources management (salaries and positions), procurement/contracts, declarations of conflicts of interest, and income and assets of public officials. Proactive disclosure provisions typically do not encompass administrative documents created in the course of conducting government operations (e.g., e-mails and other correspondence) that deal with the decision-making apparatus and related policy outcomes, which is why provisions allowing for the legal right to request government information remain relevant.

Staffing Levels

Many agencies do not devote sufficient staff time to RTI tasks, citing a lack of commitment from management or a lack of human resources. As with any organization, human resources strategies for an agency-level RTI system must anticipate training needs and turnover. External demand for information, through both information requests and proactive disclosure, will determine the number of staff necessary to meet the needs of the system. For this reason, performance monitoring of the number of requests submitted to each public body, as well as the response rate and timeliness of responses, is fundamental to understanding how to allocate human resources to the task of RTI at the organizational level.

Specialized RTI Units

There is no one model for ministry-level or public bodies that will suit all agency contexts and demands. However, there is a high degree of consensus that an information officer should be appointed within each organization to handle information requests. More effective systems operate with a principal information officer in at least each agency who is responsible for overall RTI implementation within that public body. Additional officers may be required in larger administrative units within agencies that experience higher demand or more complex requests. Table 3.6 indicates considerable variation among countries in regard to the specific arrangement regarding RTI units at the agency level.

Table 3.6 RTI Units at the Agency Level

Country	De facto unit/committee solely for RTI	Unit with RTI responsibilities if not separate RTI unit	Information officers appointed in most or all agencies
Albania	Varies by agency	Public Relations/Communication	+
India	Varies by agency	Varies	+
Jordan	−	Public Relations/Communication	−
Mexico	+	RTI Liaison Committee	+
Moldova	−	Public Relations/Communication	?
Peru	−	−	+
Romania	−	−	+
South Africa	−	−	−
Thailand	+	One-Stop Service Center	+
Uganda	−	−	−
United Kingdom	Varies by agency	FOI Unit	+
United States	Varies by agency	FOIA Unit	+
	6/12	8/12	8/12

Source: Trapnell and Lemieux 2014.
Note: FOI = freedom of information; FOIA = Freedom of Information Act; RTI = right to information.

Staff Capacity
Staff capacity is driven by adequate training and resources that allow information officers to meet their legal obligations for information disclosure.

Training
The large number of public information officers required to implement RTI systems in government bodies at the national and subnational levels, combined with the likelihood of separate provincial or state laws with different sets of rules, makes sustained centralized training difficult to implement in federal systems. The challenge of ensuring that all public information officers are trained can be further exacerbated in contexts with high levels of politicization of the public service or political instability, both of which can lead to loss of trained staff through the use of political appointments. In some countries, individual agencies have either implemented compulsory training responsibilities for their own staff, or RTI training has become embedded in local training programs, indicating that line ministries are institutionalizing RTI into regular agency functions (see table 3.7) (Alexander 2014, 574; Mizrahi and Mendiburu 2014, 103; Torres and Esquivel 2011; Trapnell 2014, 333).

In cases where individual agencies are expected to initiate and fund ongoing training, there are often few resources to do so. Even with supplemental training provided by civil society, information officers in most countries without compulsory training are operating with a low level of technical knowledge that impedes their ability to disclose information in response to information requests (Trapnell and Lemieux 2014, 39–40). Compulsory training can be accompanied by coordinated, funded efforts to incorporate RTI training into agency training programs or through centralized training efforts by national schools of public administration or enforcement bodies.

Table 3.7 Training Providers

Country	Government training providers	Training is compulsory	Additional training provided by CSOs or private sector
Albania	Training Institute for Public Administration	–	–
India	Central and state governments, Institute of Secretariat and Management	–	+
Jordan	–	–	–
Mexico	Federal Institute for Access to Information, Ministry of Public Administration, individual agencies	+	–
Moldova	–	–	+
Peru	Public Administration Secretariat, Ombudsman	–	+
Romania	–	–	+
South Africa	Ombudsman, DOJ Justice College	–	+
Thailand	Office of the Information Commission	–	–
Uganda	–	–	–
United Kingdom	Information Commissioner's Office, individual agencies	+	+
United States	Office of Information Policy, individual agencies	+	+
	8/12	3/12	7/12

Source: Trapnell and Lemieux 2014.
Note: CSO = civil society organization; DOJ = Department of Justice.

Financial and Material Resources

Lack of financial resources is cited as an obstacle to effective functioning of RTI systems both across and within countries (Trapnell and Lemieux 2014).[12] Although the absence of a specific budget line item for RTI is often considered the primary obstacle to effective RTI implementation, particularly in low-income contexts, the issue of resources is much more diffuse. RTI functions tend not to be housed in separate units dedicated to RTI, except in agencies that receive large volumes of requests, such as ministries of social welfare or pensions, or agencies that are faced with complicated classification and exception schemes, such as a ministry of defense. Thus, RTI functions are embedded in administrative functions that face common resource failures. Insufficient material resources manifest in broken, missing, or outdated equipment that impact the extent to which officials can identify and locate and reproduce information, and inadequate financial resources also can lead to low levels of staffing.

Much of the breakdown in supply of resources is not the failure of individuals or departments and is not related to RTI. It is a function of the budget cycles within government, political pressures and appointments, an overall lack of resources, and policy prioritization of different areas of government, outside the RTI domain. In the face of a lack of dedicated funding for RTI, or for lack of awareness about the extent of RTI obligations, most countries expect agencies to cover RTI costs within their existing financial envelope. An exception is the funding that is normally provided to centralized enforcement bodies, such as information commissioners.

A response to the issue of lack of resources for RTI should be rooted in a strategy that assigns greater priority for RTI funding within the existing budget and in this way is much more likely to be sustainable in the long term. This approach calls for the inclusion of RTI in regular, strategic decision making and an institutional incentive system to encourage public bodies to do so.

Staff Incentives

As noted above, policy prioritization is determined to a large extent by the level of support expressed by politicians and other government actors involved in higher levels of politics. Administrative capacity is in turn influenced by levels of this political support, facilitating prioritization of RTI at lower levels of government. This is operationalized through strategic leadership in public bodies, properly aligned incentive structures, and accountability relationships among oversight bodies, agency heads, managers, and information officers (see figure 3.1).

In terms of an RTI system, oversight relationships between managers and staff can be strengthened through formalized practices and training, in addition to performance appraisal systems that include disclosure obligations. Detrimental behavior patterns can be overcome through changes in the incentive structures so that such behavior is punished, while supportive behavior patterns are rewarded.[13] But incentive structures are complex and influenced by any number

Figure 3.1 Lines of Accountability and Responsibility That Shape Incentives

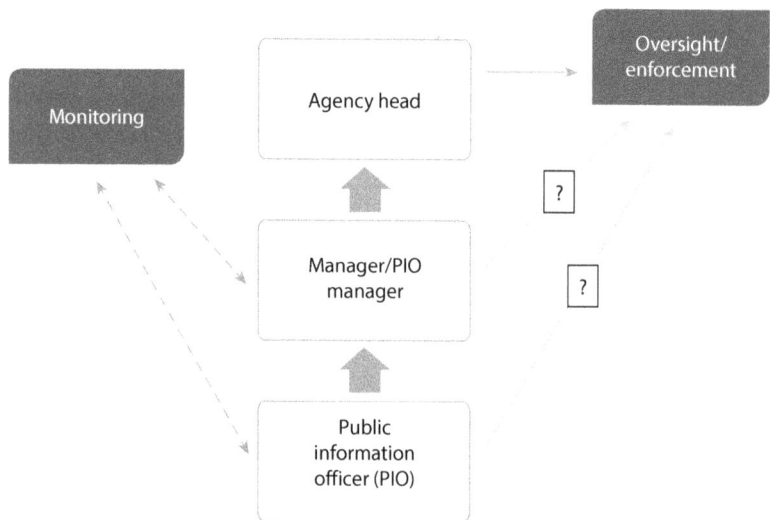

Source: Trapnell and Lemieux 2014.

of cultural norms or institutional practices. In particular, obstructive informal practices, inadequate staffing levels, and low staff capacity might need to be addressed before incentives can be properly aligned.

Incentive structures that constrain and encourage behavior are shaped by lines of accountability within agencies and across the RTI system, as shown in figure 3.1. Relationships between monitoring entities and individual agencies establish channels of communication among information officers, managers, and monitoring bodies, as shown on the left side of the diagram. This includes guidance and training provided by monitoring bodies and the reporting of requests and appeals data by individual agencies. But these relationships lack the threat of consequences unless disclosure obligations are included in monitoring responsibilities. Because accountability relationships in public sector operations rarely move diagonally from information officers to enforcement bodies, as shown on the right-hand side of the diagram, incentives must be shaped through the horizontal accountability relationships between agency heads and information officers, and between agency heads and enforcement bodies.[14] Although chief information officers may be responsible for the operational activities associated with RTI, agency heads are the locus of accountability in RTI implementation, making leadership at all levels a key component in shaping attitudes and behavior and prioritizing RTI policy.

It is likely that there is a significant and positive relationship between a professionalized civil service and properly aligned staff incentives that affect RTI implementation. This implies that appropriate incentives employed in the public sector may have a significant effect on RTI effectiveness at the agency level. These incentives include appropriate time for additional duties, functioning personnel evaluations with accurate measurement, protection of staff for good faith disclosures, and a lack of formal or informal penalties for disclosing information, such as penalties for improper disclosure or protection for good faith disclosures. Training specific to RTI obligations, including records management, also contributes to encouraging appropriate behavior. The fact that no country in the sample of countries we studied mentioned the need for special rewards such as cash bonuses or administrative honors suggests that properly aligned incentives matter more for motivating behavior than special rewards.

Institutional capacity, referring to the specialist and nonspecialist functions of government operations, such as records management, strategic planning, budgeting and personnel management, and monitoring progress toward goals, is a major determinant of effective RTI law implementation. Weak or ineffective RTI implementation is often the result of a lack of updated and formal practices for request processing, records management and proactive disclosure of information, insufficient staff capacity, lack of financial resources, and weak staff incentives to support RTI implementation. Many of these problems are linked to weak institutional capacity across government as a whole, including weak leadership and the absence of a professionalized civil service. Effective monitoring and oversight of RTI implementation, discussed in the next section, can help identify and address these implementation issues.

Section 4: Oversight

Oversight consists of both monitoring tasks and enforcement responsibilities. Monitoring tasks include management of nationwide implementation and guidance on the design of policies at the national, subnational, and agency levels, while enforcement responsibilities include decision processes on appeals and complaints, and enforcement of appropriate sanctions for noncompliance.[15]

Strong RTI systems benefit from effective management during implementation that facilitates adequate resources and resolution of administrative delays. Although legal frameworks may clearly specify the enforcement mechanisms for an RTI system, the institutional arrangements for monitoring of implementation may be set through de facto practices in the public sector. Information commissioners are often tasked with a number of implementation responsibilities but can contribute effective solutions pertaining to implementation only to the degree of their authority and independence to act (see box 3.6) (Holsen and Pasquier 2012).

Monitoring Responsibilities and Institutional Arrangements

For effective and consistent implementation of RTI across ministries and agencies, it is important that at least one national-level authority is made responsible for supporting the implementation process, often by articulating a framework for RTI implementation. This body is often referred to as a "nodal authority," and its role is to assist agencies by performing an integrating and coordinating function, for example, in setting up appropriate organizational structures and administrative procedures that facilitate compliance with the law.

A few countries have some provision for the establishment of the nodal authority in the RTI law, but there are also cases (e.g., India) where no such

---

Box 3.6 Independence of Oversight

Five key aspects of an information commissioner's formal independence are (1) whether the independence of the body is explicitly granted by law; (2) appointment of the commissioner; (3) the length of a commissioner's term; (4) dismissal of the commissioner; and (5) who funds the oversight body.

Formal—or *de jure*—independence is that which an organization possesses by law:

- It is important to politicians because it sets parameters for control over the regulator; for example, it sets guidelines for removing the head of a regulating body; and
- It matters to the regulators because it provides legal protection, for example, from arbitrary dismissal when they issue an unpopular decision or recommendation.

Informal—or *de facto*—independence describes the autonomy an institution has in its day-to-day functioning. It entails independence in practice, rather than in law, and includes such dimensions as resourcing and leadership.

Source: Summary of Holsen and Pasquier 2012, 229–30.

---

provision exists. In general, for a non-rulemaking central coordinating and support role, there is no particular need for the nodal authority to be established in the law or even in regulations under the law to operate effectively, as long as it has some real authority (of whatever kind, and this could be quite diverse, including political). That said, it is preferable to establish the nodal authority in law to provide it with a strong legal basis for existence and to bolster its legitimacy.

There are diverse arrangements for the placement of nodal responsibilities, for example, some in government bodies such as justice ministries, some with committee structures, and others where responsibility is decentralized across two agencies (see appendix C). In several countries with the highest RTI scores, the nodal responsibility rests with an agency responsible for public administration. However, we emphasize the need to consider the most effective placement in terms of where real authority rests in the country context.

There are also cases where, because of its authority within government or powers under the law, the enforcement body (e.g., an information commissioner's office or an ombudsman) takes on some of the nodal functions. In South Africa, for example, the Human Rights Commission issues reports, develops a public guide, undertakes public education, conducts training, etc., even though it sits outside of government. In Mexico, as well, the oversight body (Instituto Federal de Acceso a la Información [Federal Institute for Access to Information]) does an enormous amount of promotional work, both externally (i.e., with the public) and inside government. This approach may be taken where a nodal function within the executive branch of government is weak or nonexistent.

There is a range of RTI monitoring responsibilities that are assumed by public bodies, including the issuance of implementing rules, performance monitoring, training oversight, public outreach, issuance of guidance and/or best practice models, and publication of recommendations to policy makers. Nodal agencies often share some of these responsibilities with enforcement bodies or other ministries within government. But, in the absence of effective interagency cooperation, such institutional arrangements may increase the likelihood that implementation processes will vary in quality and pace. Appendix C provides a snapshot of the institutional arrangements for a sample of 12 countries with RTI laws.

Regardless of the institutional arrangements, any agencies assigned monitoring responsibilities must be adequately resourced and hold sufficient authority within government (see table 3.8). Without guidance and logistical supervision, there is a significant likelihood that implementing rules and regulations will be inconsistent, particularly when responsibility for developing these rules is left to individual agencies. Weak monitoring efforts also hamper implementation processes, particularly when agencies cannot be compelled to improve their RTI practices.

Enforcement Mechanisms

Although monitoring efforts may consist of reviewing compliance, providing training, and issuing guidance or internal rules on implementation, enforcement has to do with ensuring compliance with RTI laws. Enforcement includes the

Table 3.8 Monitoring Responsibilities Performed by Nodal Authorities or Enforcement Bodies

Country	Issuance of implementing rules	Performance monitoring	Training provision/ Training oversight	Public outreach	Issuance of best practice models/ guidance	Publishing recommendations to policy makers
Albania	–	–	+	–	–	–
India	+	+	+	+	+	–
Jordan	–	–	–	–	–	–
Mexico	+	+	+	+	+	+
Moldova	–	–	–	–	–	–
Peru	+	?	+	+	?	+
Romania	+	–	–	–	–	–
South Africa	–	+	+	+	+	–
Thailand	+	–	+	–	–	+
Uganda	–	–	–	–	–	–
United Kingdom	+	+	+	–	+	+
United States	–	+	+	–	+	+
	6/12	6/12	8/12	4/12	6/12	5/12

Source: Trapnell and Lemieux 2014.

hearing of appeals, investigation of complaints, issuance of binding resolutions, and recommendations for sanctions.

Appeals are formal requests to a higher authority for a reversal of an official decision or to require a decision to be made. In RTI systems, they can also be filed for other reasons, such as failure to respond within a time limit or charging unreasonable fees, but this depends on the conditions specified in the RTI law. If the requester continues to seek a reversal of the original decision, appeals can progress through several levels of authority in many countries until they reach the judiciary. Decisions on appeals may or may not be binding, depending on the institutional mandate of the organization making the decision, such as courts versus information commissioners.

The availability of appeals systems and ways in which requesters can appeal refusals to grant information vary by country. Most countries have multistage appeals systems that start with an internal appeal at the agency level. If the requester is not satisfied with the response, the next stage is usually an external appeal at an information commission or an administrative tribunal. These bodies can vary in their authority to issue binding decisions, but many are able to compel the release of information from public bodies. When external appeals authorities do not exist, or when lack of access to information cannot be appealed by law, requesters can file complaints with grievance redress bodies. These bodies offer mediation services but cannot compel disclosure through binding adjudication.[16]

However, some information commissions and/or commissioners undertake an adjudicative (i.e. nonmediation) function but still cannot issue binding orders.

Distinctions can be made between mediation and adjudication, and then within the latter, between binding and nonbinding order powers.

As shown in table 3.9, some countries have a very limited appeals process before the final appeal in the courts.

Countries vary in the complexity of the appeals process, and assessment of effectiveness in appeals depends very much on the practices of individual bodies and the nature of information requests. Delays in appeals at the judicial level are common across countries. Combined with a lack of faith in judicial capacity or rule of law, delays and cost may contribute to a reluctance to pursue appeals through the courts.

The existence of an information commissioner or comparable enforcement body in an RTI system allows for a second level of appeal outside the public body or the courts, one that does not require legal representation. In addition, information commissions, if well resourced and mandated with appropriate independent authority, can employ alternative methods of enforcement besides

Table 3.9 Levels of Appeals Process

Country	Internal appeals process at the agency level	External administrative appeals authority (binding decisions)	Appeals submitted to courts	Grievance redress for RTI complaints (mediation)
Albania	+	−	+	People's Advocate (Ombudsman)
India	+	Central Information Commission/State Information Commissions	+	Central Information Commission/State Information Commissions
Jordan	−	Information Council (possibly not binding)	+	−
Mexico	+	Information Commission (IFAI)	+	Information Commission (IFAI)
Moldova	+	−	+	−
Peru	+	−	+	Office of Public Defender (Ombudsman)
Romania	+	−	+	People's Advocate (Ombudsman)
South Africa	+	−	+	Human Rights Commission
Thailand	−	Information Disclosure Tribunal	+	Office of the Information Commission
Uganda	+	−	+	Human Rights Commission
United Kingdom	+	Information Commissioner's Office	+	Information Commissioner's Office
United States	+	−	+	Office of Government Information Services
	10/12	5/12	12/12	10/12

Source: Trapnell and Lemieux 2014.
Note: RTI = right to information.

appeals and sanctions. As shown in table 3.10, enforcement bodies can employ persuasive techniques based on the extent of their authority. These approaches include conducting closed-door meetings, issuing notices of inquiry with threat of inspection, publishing compulsory guidelines or analyses of specific RTI challenges, or calling senior officials as witnesses in investigations. The mission of ombudsmen often does not extend to this type of intervention, and existing nodal bodies may or may not have the capacity or authority to conduct these kinds of activities.

Sanctions may be important as a remote threat, but findings from the 12 case studies question whether a *credible* threat of sanctions is prevalent across RTI frameworks, because even where sanctions are available they are very rarely applied in most countries. This suggests that the possibility of penalties is not necessarily the primary means of enforcement in RTI systems. Aside from the need for an effective appeals process, which is a necessary but not sufficient means of enforcement in RTI systems, no clear pattern emerges about what works best for enforcement. It may well be that a combination of methods works most effectively to enforce disclosure obligations, particularly when capitalizing on the stronger institutions and norms of individual countries. These institutions and norms may include a strong judicial system, a tradition of consistent application of rules by government bodies, active and respected CSOs that can influence change within government, or the potential for collaboration between public bodies and oversight agencies.

Table 3.10 Enforcement Methods

Country	Effective appeals process (including courts)	Binding decisions by enforcement body	Possibility of sanctions or fines (by IC or courts)	Persuasion/ monitoring/ investigation	Public release of data on poor performance
Albania	−	−	−	−	−
India	+	+	+	+	+
Jordan	−	?	−	−	−
Mexico	+	+	+	+	+
Moldova	−	−	−	−	−
Peru	+	−	+	+	+
Romania	+	−	+	−	−
South Africa	+	−	−	−	+
Thailand	+	+	−	−	−
Uganda	−	−	−	−	−
United Kingdom	+	+	+	+	+
United States	+	−	+	+	+
	8/12	4/12	6/12	5/12	6/12

Source: Trapnell and Lemieux 2014.

Note: IC = Information commission or other external public body.

Third-Party Oversight Mechanisms

Although the primary responsibility for oversight of RTI implementation rests with the government, there are also opportunities for external actors to reinforce the importance of monitoring and enforcement capabilities. Regional instruments can play an influential role in both areas, by providing targeted guidance to countries about strengths and weaknesses in their RTI systems, while also encouraging governments to adopt specific practices that may improve the functioning of RTI implementation.

As an example, the African Commission on Human and Peoples' Rights has been able to influence country actions through its recommendations on implementation. Uganda was asked to issue regulations in 2010 and reported compliance in 2014. Recently Angola accepted the Universal Periodic Report recommendation on amending and effectively implementing its RTI law. In Latin America and Europe, regional instruments function as legal watchdogs and regional human rights courts. The Office of the Special Rapporteur for Freedom of Expression, under the Inter-American Commission on Human Rights, publishes guidance on legal frameworks and implementation issues specific to Latin American countries. The Inter-American Court of Human Rights, as the judicial institution of the Organization of American States, has set regional precedent in RTI cases by ruling in favor of RTI in member countries. The European Court of Human Rights has also played a prominent role in the evolution of RTI in European countries. The ASEAN Intergovernmental Commission on Human Rights, operating in East Asian countries, has recently recognized the RTI, but work on this issue area has been slow to progress.

In addition to regional instruments that can bring about pressure at the political level, CSOs often engage in monitoring of implementation processes at the organizational and municipal level to encourage governments to better understand how RTI is functioning in practice. In both cases cited above with the African Commission on Human and Peoples' Rights, local organizations such as the Africa Freedom of Information Centre (AFIC) have been involved in shadow reporting and engaging these mechanisms to put pressure on countries. There is also the possibility that CSOs will engage in primary research on their own. Often this takes the form of compliance or field testing of information request processing, which involves documenting the time and difficulty involved in accessing information through official request procedures. In more than half of the countries from the underlying research for this guide, CSOs conduct compliance testing on the rates and quality of response from government. This kind of data can be compared to self-reported data from administrative systems to provide a more accurate understanding of agency performance. However, it is rare for governments to recognize and utilize this information in their planning efforts. This is a lost opportunity, because such information can be used to provide a fuller understanding of RTI in practice, as well as promote collaboration between government and civil society that could provide efficiency gains to organizations.

Section 5: Transformative Factors—Collaboration, Technology, and Interagency Cooperation

Some features of RTI systems extend across the four domains of RTI implementation yet are not always included in the narratives of success and failure. They fall into no single domain exclusively, but instead influence the path of each driver in different ways. These *transformative factors* have the potential to enhance aspects of the drivers significantly by increasing their efficiency, efficacy, and inclusiveness, thus magnifying their impact.

State-Society Collaboration

Advocacy efforts refer to contestation over the institutionalization of rights, which by their nature are subject to challenge and transformation by stakeholders. Human rights, in fact, stand in opposition to the arbitrary use of power and privilege (Stammers 2009, 105). Civil debate over the shape of legal instruments or the path of implementation allows for the balance of interests from both government and society and is a natural part of inclusive governance (Cohen and Arato 1994). Once rights become embedded in structures of administrative power, thereby reducing the distance between state and citizen, there is also space for collaboration over the direction of policies and implementing rules (Booth 2012).

State-society collaboration refers to engagement between civil society and the government that is not considered adversarial. This includes working groups, stakeholder consultations, and participation in committees and councils. It ranges from joint efforts to produce outcomes, which may include civil servant training and promotional activities for the public, to solicitation of civil society feedback, such as on the relevance of proactively disclosed information. Formalized means of collaboration are important for sustainability purposes, but governments must be able to see the value of joint efforts in RTI systems for institutionalization of these practices to occur.

CSOs and media play a major role in all aspects of implementation in the sample countries, even if their absolute numbers are small. These activities range from training to compliance monitoring and public outreach, with CSOs substantially represented in these activities. Countries at various levels of GDP and extent of RTI implementation benefit from civil society involvement in the training of public officials (e.g., India, Moldova, Peru, Romania, South Africa, the United Kingdom, and the United States), suggesting that civil society groups are in close collaboration with government in the planning of training or in assisting in government-sponsored RTI training efforts (Alexander 2014; Devasher Surie and Aiyar 2014; Mizrahi and Mendiburu 2014; Moses 2014; Pereira Chumbe 2014; Trapnell 2014). In India and Mexico, CSOs are regularly invited to provide input into policies and legal amendments (Devasher Surie and Aiyar 2014; Mizrahi and Mendiburu 2014). CSOs in Jordan have proposed that nongovernmental organizations be given seats on the information council (Meknassi 2014, 387).

There are also instances in which the civic space does not yet allow for meaningful collaboration between public officials and civil society. In Albania, civil society groups or citizens have few opportunities to engage with highly centralized decision-making processes (Trebicka and Shella 2014, 13). The civil society sector in Moldova lacks institutional capacity and, often, basic equipment, and polarization of the media has called the independence of the press into question (Lipcean and Stefan 2014, 168). The small community of CSOs and journalists working on RTI in Jordan operates in a politically conservative environment with sporadic opportunities for substantive engagement (Meknassi 2014, 395). In these contexts, considerable distance exists between state and citizenry, suggesting that traditional principal–agent models of RTI operation remain relevant, although the RTI area naturally lends itself to such models. Collaborative efforts between civil society and government are predicated upon a shared concern for establishing sustainable and meaningful aspects of open government, from training to public awareness, accessibility, and responsiveness.

CSOs and the media focus on a variety of areas regarding transparency, and they play important participatory roles in RTI implementation. Engagement by civil society on issues related to RTI implementation matter for RTI effectiveness, although no particular form of engagement has emerged as being more or less important. However, the effects of participation and collaboration are complex and nonlinear. A recent study on participation and development outcomes showed that a budget participation subindex constructed from items on the Open Budget Index[17] did not predict development outcomes or expenditure levels. A possible explanation suggested by the authors is that the indicators used in the subindex on participation reflected only possible engagement opportunities, not actual engagement (Fukuda-Parr, Guyer, and Lawson-Remer 2011). These findings confirm that questions about the quality and extent of civil society engagement remain unanswered, even though there is general agreement that civil society participation matters for effective policy implementation.[18] At a minimum, public bodies and governments can engage in consultative processes with CSOs to identify information that is in high public demand and relevant for users' needs, which will ultimately enhance the overall functioning of the RTI system.

Technology

Technology is a tool that augments success, but it does not solve problems automatically. It is often touted as a solution to issues of efficiency and easy access to services. In terms of transparency, for example, online submission of requests allows government to track the status of RTI requests and collect data automatically, obviating the need for public officials to log requests. Such systems also make it vastly easier for at least citizens with online access to make requests. Web portals are the main mechanism for dissemination of proactively disclosed information, providing access to documents to a wide audience. Technology-enabled forms of recorded communication, such as e-mail and text, can increase the efficient flow of information throughout government. But the success of technology is based on a clear understanding of the needs and interests of users, both internal and external to government, the capacity of those users to employ technology effectively and sustainably, the provision of human and material resources to support the introduction and maintenance of technology solutions, and the way that technology is used to create and maintain recorded communications.

Although it is true that technological approaches to transparency can quickly facilitate access and openness, significant human and technical capital is the bedrock upon which technology rests. With few exceptions, technology for transparency and accountability purposes is rarely adopted across-the-board to universal acclaim. For instance, in terms of the claim that technology facilitates easier access to information, it is more likely that successful technological approaches are tailored to the needs of various user communities (Fung, Gilman, and Shkabatur 2010). Parents of school-age children, for example, may be very interested in online information about school fees, curricula, and teaching quality. Online information on medical treatments and hospital quality may be valuable to patients, doctors, and otherwise healthy individuals. Interventions that are successful on this kind of large scale tend to organize and display information that is immediately relevant to users' lives and provide access to information in easily accessible formats. Other technological interventions may complement mainstream efforts at transparency by releasing specialized information that is relevant for intermediaries, such as journalists or political campaigners, who then make the information accessible to a wider audience. Ultimately the most successful use of technology for transparency purposes may lie with interventions that are dedicated to advancing the agendas of CSOs (Fung, Gilman, and Shkabatur 2010). Examples of this type include budget tracking tools, crowdsourcing of information via mobile phones, and online platforms for submission of complaints and requests. In addition, as noted previously in the discussion on records management, far from improving access and openness, in some cases, increased reliance on ICTs within the public sector has decreased the quality of information disclosed. Thus, technology, though a transformative factor, may not necessarily transform situations for the better without sufficient capacity, resources, planning and attention to the issues mentioned above (Lemieux 2016; World Bank 2016).

Intragovernmental Collaboration

Collaboration between records management authorities, technology departments, and nodal authorities or monitoring bodies is an important means of embedding RTI successfully into administrative operations, with the aim of making information disclosure a business-as-usual process. Increasingly, the approach to managing recorded communication, regardless of the physical medium of creation or storage or of the creator of the information and administrative body responsible for its management, is referred to as information governance.[19] In the countries we studied, little evidence is found of collaboration between technology officers and RTI officials, and in some cases, responsibility for proactive disclosure practices is held among individual departments, the heads of public bodies, and communities of practice, with technology staff even outside of the discussion in some cases.[20] Moreover, communities of practice or networks of practitioners across public bodies are relatively rare. Collaboration between different technical units, however, can facilitate both dialogue and practical decision making over RTI responsibilities, while the creation of communities of practice among RTI officials encourages sharing of good practices and knowledge about RTI responsibilities, in addition to contributing to efficiency within government.

These transformative factors—state-society collaboration, technology, and intragovernmental collaboration—may not directly contribute to improved outcomes, but they serve as instrumental supports for the RTI system as a whole. In addition, their impacts reverberate throughout the implementation process. Rather than boosting implementation effectiveness in one big push, transformative factors can build on, enhance, and sustain efforts to support RTI implementation.

Section 6: Sequencing Implementation and Strengthening Components

In the previous chapters, we have discussed the components that drive effective RTI law implementation. In any well-functioning RTI regime, all of these components will be present and operating effectively. An open question remains, however: in what order or sequence should these components be implemented? Relatedly, are there some components that must always be in place before the other components can operate effectively, or is it possible for an RTI regime to operate effectively even without some of these components?

The first point to be made about sequencing of RTI implementation is that there is no proven theory of it in relation to the effectiveness of RTI. Instead, for now we must rely upon general theories of sequencing in the study of international development, expert opinion, and anecdotal evidence derived from case studies and actual experience. These sources can offer useful pointers to the possible sequencing of actions to be taken when implementing RTI laws, though there exists no clear evidence that one approach is necessarily more universally effective than another.

General Theories

Brian Levy has written about initiating development and possible early-stage interventions in his book *Working with the Grain*. Though Levy does not dwell upon the specific question of RTI implementation, he does discuss what he thinks should be the focus of development in each of four country typologies. For example, for the "dominant discretionary" trajectory, the top-down developmental state, he suggests a focus on expanding bureaucratic capability without the openness of the political system (Levy 2014, 33). For countries that fit this typology, focusing on strengthening RTI institutional capacity, such as records management systems, could be a successful strategy in that this could prepare the way for a freer flow of information when conditions in such a country allow for fuller disclosure of information. It is also possible that in such regimes, early efforts to encourage proactive disclosure of information (e.g., information focused upon service improvements or disclosure of information relating to specific sectors) may provide an entry point or stepping stone to the establishment of a later legal RTI. Along these lines, Levy notes that Ethiopia's use of bottom-up monitoring of service quality created space for critical discussion (39). Moreover, "Subsequently, if early-stage discretionary dominance is successfully traversed, then a new set of frontier challenges will come to the fore. The middle-class is likely to grow, bringing with it rising civic demands for openness" (42). Research still is needed to determine whether there are actually countries that have followed this hypothetical development pathway to effective implementation of RTI and, if so, how effective their RTI implementation efforts have subsequently been.

For countries along the "rule-of-law competitive" trajectory to sustainable development, Levy states that political leaders need to strike bargains and gain the support of nonelites in order to maintain stability. In such cases, far-reaching policy reforms to improve the public sector will be low on the agenda, and Levy therefore suggests that strengthening CSOs can generate pressures for improvements in state institutions (Levy 2014, 37). In regard to institutional improvements, Levy counsels keeping these focused and targeted toward binding constraints, rather than being comprehensive (41).

Though Levy suggests clear predilections or starting points for countries of particular types, he is also careful to point out that "A 'with-the-grain' approach to reform builds on strengths, works around constraints, and leverages the momentum of governance-growth interactions to keep the process moving forward" (Levy 2014, 40). For this reason, the above starting points should not be viewed as absolute but as indicative. The wisest course is likely to involve an assessment of current RTI effectiveness to identify areas where preparation for implementation is needed and to explore opportunities for improvement.

Indeed, a more incremental approach to development has gained favor recently. Andrews, Pritchett, and Woolcock (2012) stress the importance of solving problems, not selling solutions. They argue that development efforts should begin by asking "what is the problem?" instead of "which solution should we adopt?" and call for a "problem driven iterative adaptation" approach. The problem-driven iterative adaptation (PDIA) approach is characterized by reform activity that aims to do the following:

1. Solve particular problems in particular local contexts,
2. Create an "authorizing environment" for decision making that encourages experimentation and "positive deviance," which gives rise to
3. Active, ongoing, and experiential (and experimental) learning and the iterative feedback of lessons into new solutions, doing so by

4. Engaging broad sets of agents to ensure that reforms are viable, legitimate, and relevant—that is, are politically supportable and practically implementable (Andrews, Pritchett, and Woolcock, 2012, 8).

Following this approach, the implementation of RTI would proceed with identification of a particular problem in the local context. This may be, for example, the need to improve service delivery or to improve the country's investment climate. This approach has the added advantage of clearly articulating who the beneficiaries of the RTI law should be and thus of creating a framework for later measurement and evaluation of RTI implementation initiatives based on feedback from beneficiaries.

Expert Opinion

In addition to drawing upon ideas from development theories to guide decisions about sequencing implementation of RTI laws, the opinions of the many experts who have had to implement RTI laws within their own jurisdictions may also be relied upon. Much can be learned from the steps they have taken to implement RTI laws.

The Commonwealth Human Rights Initiative identifies training of public officials, raising public awareness, proactive disclosure, and records management as among the areas that typically need to be addressed early on in RTI implementation (Commonwealth Human Rights Initiative n.d.). Carole Excell has prepared a list of the top 10 things to do in the first six months of implementing an RTI law based on a review of a number of implementation plans that have been prepared by governments around the world and her own experience of leading the implementation of the Cayman Islands' Freedom of Information Act (see box 3.7) (Excell 2011).

Appendix A provides a list of publications prepared by the U.K. and Scottish information commissioners concerning the types and sequencing of activities needed to support the implementation of RTI laws.

Case Studies

Implementing RTI can seem like an overwhelming task for any country, let alone those that are resource constrained. An analysis of implementation practice indicates that many countries therefore tackle RTI implementation by adopting a phased approach. In some countries, such as Canada, Jamaica, South Africa, and the United Kingdom, the law was brought into force in phases to allow agencies time to prepare properly for implementation. Some jurisdictions have also taken a phased approach to bringing agency RTI systems "online." In Jamaica, for example, implementation focused on groups of public bodies based on anticipated demand (Livingstone 2005, 2015). The United Kingdom also initially adopted a phased approach to implementation, starting with central departments, followed by local government, and finally semiautonomous administrations, such as the National Health Service and the police services. This phased-in

---

Box 3.7 Implementation of a Freedom of Information Law: Top 10 Things to Do in the First Six Months

1. Set up a Freedom of Information Implementation Unit (decide on leadership, recruitment, budget, role, reporting).
2. Set up a Freedom of Information Coordination/Steering Committee with representation across government with responsibility to give progress reports on implementation, develop action plans, and address the special needs of specified agencies, IT, training, records management, public participation, etc.
3. Launch the commencement of the implementation process—awareness raising and introduction of FOI to government and to the public (introduction to chief officers, heads of agencies, civil servants, public events, Cabinet, etc.).
4. Conduct a baseline assessment of the state of preparedness of government agencies (records management), complete an analysis of current record management and retrieval systems, identifying changes required and providing advice to Chief Officer and agencies, and prepare an FOI questionnaire to understand readiness to implement new FOI regulations.
5. Create job description and designation of Information Managers (circular from chief secretary on policy for hiring/budget for positions) for each agency and creation of information managers network.
6. Create government-wide implementation plan, public consultation on plan, and sign-off by Cabinet.
7. Create a list of all public authorities (ministerial/chief officers, contacts, telephone and fax numbers, e-mail addresses).
8. Undertake analysis of the public's need for FOI and types of service delivery—what type of information do they need, what type of requests are they likely to make, how can it be made easier for them, are they worried about having persons know about their requests (confidentiality), what are their expectations come the start of the FOI regime. Conduct focus groups/surveys to ensure that implementation meets the needs of the public.
9. Create model public authority plans and implementation.
10. Develop consultation paper on policy issues to be resolved by FOI regulations and process for review of sectoral laws.

Source: Excell 2011.
Note: FOI = freedom of information; IT = information technology.

---

introduction of the law was abandoned in late 2001, however, when a decision was made at the central political level to implement the law across the whole of the public sector in a single, so-called big bang on January 1, 2005. According to reports, the big bang approach had a number of negative consequences for implementation of the act, some of which were not overcome until 2010. Among these were delays in handling complaints by the Information Commissioner's Office (Trapnell 2014).

A common theme in the case studies, also supported by scholarly literature on RTI implementation, is the importance of the nodal and oversight bodies (e.g., an authority within the executive branch of government or an independent information commissioner's office, depending on the jurisdiction) in initiating and subsequently driving implementation (see, for example, Holsen and Pesquier 2012). In almost all countries that we studied, a nodal authority has taken the first steps toward implementation by formulating an implementation plan and working with public agencies to strengthen capacity and with civil society to raise awareness. This draws attention to the value of establishing the monitoring and oversight body or bodies and quickly bringing it (them) into effective operation as a first order of business.

Case studies point to most of the early focus in RTI implementation being on strengthening institutional capacity. Training of information officers, sensitization sessions for general staff, formation of networks of information officers across government, and development of guidelines and informational publications are all mentioned as activities that have been undertaken at the earliest stages of RTI implementation. However, some countries have undertaken a review of laws that conflict with the RTI law as a first step, which can be a positive measure to combat entrenched cultures of secrecy. Other countries have undertaken public awareness campaigns (e.g., Jamaica). In Canada, where public education was not carried out when the law was first introduced, very low request rates resulted. This can create a dangerous dynamic if officials have been specially recruited and trained, and if public agencies have put resources into RTI preparedness in anticipation of high demand. Low initial demand may lead to the loss of qualified staff and to dissipation of support and resources, as happened in the United Kingdom. This suggests the need to strike a careful balance between building institutional capacity and encouraging public demand for information in the early stages of RTI implementation.

A review of the available evidence suggests that there is no one path to implementation that guarantees an effective RTI law, though this conclusion is made without the benefit of a strong theoretical framework to underpin sequencing activities relating to RTI implementation. It appears, however, that the sequencing of activities needed to bring an RTI law into effect depends, in part, upon the unique circumstances of each country. In some, there may be weak political will and entrenched cultures of secrecy generating resistance to the law. In other cases, public awareness and the demand for information may be low. In still others, institutional capacity to implement the law may be weak because of a lack of trained staff or weak records management. An early stage assessment of RTI implementation effectiveness can help to identify areas needing particular attention. Whatever the circumstances in a given context, sufficient evidence supports the value, as Andrews, Pritchett, and Woolcock (2012) suggest, of engaging broad sets of agents to ensure that reforms are viable, legitimate, and relevant; that is, they are politically supportable and practically implementable.

Notes

1. We mean political stability not in the sense of political status, but rather in the sense of stable governance, as indicated by "the traditions and institutions by which authority in a country is exercised. This includes the process by which governments are selected, monitored and replaced; the capacity of the government to effectively formulate and implement sound policies; and the respect of citizens and the state for the institutions that govern economic and social interactions among them" (World Bank, Worldwide Governance Indicators, http://info.worldbank.org/governance/wgi/index.aspx#home).

2. The EEI is a global composite index developed using secondary data that seeks to understand the propensity of citizens to participate in civil society. It is made up of 71 secondary statistical data sources that are clustered into 53 indicators. To be incorporated into the EEI, scores are reweighted on a scale of 0–1, with 0 being least enabling and 1 being most enabling.

3. It should be noted that evidence for this finding is recent and yet to be replicated outside of the underlying research for this guide.

4. It should be noted that study of political support for RTI implementation is limited by a lack of systematic evidence. Conclusions in this guide are based on scholarly research and extensive primary research over a two-year period; however, results have not yet been replicated.

5. Funding of RTI implementation activities is also not necessarily tied to donor support. As per Trapnell and Lemieux (2014), international funding or technical assistance seems to correlate closely with the level of GDP, rather than with types of implementation activities or demonstrated policy prioritization.

6. Often information requests are submitted by urban professionals working in the field of government information and transparency. These kinds of specialists are able to devote significantly more time to understanding RTI rules and processes and to securing funding for lengthy appeals.

7. In some contexts, communication over the nature of an information request may proceed as a collaborative focusing of the request, whereas in other more adversarial contexts, it may proceed as a formal negotiation.

8. Note that the definition of records in ISO 15489 differs from definitions of records or information that one might find in an RTI law, where generally it is better to have very broad definitions so that more material is in the scope of the law than excluded from it.

9. ISO15489 (2001).

10. The International Records Management Trust has for years documented the weak state of records management in developing countries (see, for example, International Records Management Trust 2010–2011.

11. See, for example, National Security Archive, White House E-Mail, http://nsarchive.gwu.edu/white_house_email/.

12. In a thematic analysis of 12 country case studies, nearly all countries cited issues with lack of financial, human, and material resources, regardless of strength of the RTI system or country income level.

13. Fox and Haight (2011) refer to issues of values on the one hand, and interests and power on the other. This guide takes the view that addressing interests and power within administrative contexts can contribute to changes in the attitudes of public officials.

14. Fox and Haight (2011) note that the internal audit units embedded within Mexican public bodies are responsible to the supreme audit institution, establishing a diagonal relationship between audit officers and the audit oversight body. This may be an option to insert additional means of accountability within RTI systems.

15. Other conceptions of oversight differentiate between internal monitoring, which is related to the management of implementation but not of guidance or most of the other roles performed by nodal bodies, and external monitoring, as in assessment of compliance by an external body.

16. It should be noted that grievance redress through the ombudsman does not result in binding decisions, but rather channels complaints through a mediation process in the hope that public bodies will disclose information in lieu of appeals.

17. The Open Budget Index examines budget transparency, participation, and oversight for more than 100 countries. This includes the types of information that are made available to the public and kinds of opportunities to engage with officials over the content of budget documents.

18. Recent studies on e-participation reveal that the outcomes of citizen engagement, where individuals feel that their actions ultimately influenced government decision making, are correlated with higher perceptions of government responsiveness and transparency (Kim and Lee 2012).

19. Kooper Maes, and Lindgreen (2011) state that information governance involves establishing an environment and opportunities, rules, and decision-making rights for the valuation, creation, collection, analysis, distribution, storage, use, and control of information; it answers the question "What information do we need, how do we make use of it, and who is responsible for it?" They note that information governance was introduced scientifically by Donaldson and Walker (2004) as a framework to support the work at the National Health Society on security and confidentiality arrangements to apply at multiple levels in electronic information services. More recently, a report was published by the Economist Intelligence Unit (2008) on the use of information governance in enterprises. Information governance in these approaches typically includes records management, privacy regulation, information security, data flows and ownership, and data life cycle management.

20. A good example of this issue is seen in the handling of open data initiatives, which may not be coordinated with authorities responsible for RTI. For a discussion on this issue, see Devasher Surie and Aiyar (2014, 75).

References

Alexander, Shannon. 2014. "Implementing Right to Information: A Case Study of the United States." In *Right to Information: Case Studies on Implementation*, edited by Stephanie E. Trapnell, 539–624. Right to Information Series. Washington, DC: World Bank. http://siteresources.worldbank.org/PUBLICSECTORANDGOVERNANCE /Resources/285741-1343934891414/8787489-1344020463266/8788935 -1399321576201/RTI_Case_Studies_Implementation_WEBfinal.pdf.

Andrews, Matt, Lant Pritchett, and Michael Woolcock. 2012. "Escaping Capability Traps through Problem-Driven Iterative Adaptation (PDIA)." Working Paper 299, Center for Global Development, Washington, DC. http://www.cgdev.org/publication/escaping -capability-traps-through-problem-driven-iterative-adaptation-pdia-working-paper.

Berliner, Daniel, and Aaron Erlich. 2015. "Competing for Transparency: Political Competition and Institutional Reform in Mexican States." *American Political Science Review* 109 (1): 110–28.

Booth, David. 2012. "The Centrality of Collective Action Problems in Governance for Development: New Evidence." Governance for Development, World Bank, Washington, DC. https://blogs.worldbank.org/governance/the-centrality-of-collective -action-problems-in-governance-for-development-new-evidence.

Cambridge Economic Associates and PDG South Africa. 2014. *Disclosure of Information in Public Private Partnerships*. Washington, DC: World Bank Institute.

Carter Center. 2014a. *Access to Information Implementation Assessment Tool*. http://www .cartercenter.org/peace/ati/IAT/index.html.

———. 2014b. *Women and the Right of Access to Information in Liberia: A Mixed-Methods Study*. Atlanta: Carter Center. http://www.cartercenter.org/resources/pdfs/peace/ati /women-and-ati-prepub-07172014.pdf.

Centre for Freedom of Information. 2014. *In the Experience of Information Commissioners: The Information Commissioners' International Exchange Network Survey 2014*. http://www.centrefoi.org.uk/edocs/pdfs/centrfoi_survey_november _2014.pdf.

Cohen, Jean L., and Andrew Arato. 1994. *Civil Society and Political Theory*. Cambridge, MA: MIT Press.

Commonwealth Human Rights Initiative. n.d. "Right to Information: Preparing for Implementation." http://www.humanrightsinitiative.org/programs/ai/rti/implementation /preparing_for_implementation.htm.

Devasher Surie, Mandakini, and Yamini Aiyar. 2014. "Implementing Right to Information: A Case Study of India." In *Right to Information: Case Studies on Implementation*, edited by Stephanie E. Trapnell, 49–102. Right to Information Series. Washington, DC: World Bank. http://siteresources.worldbank.org/PUBLICSECTORANDGOVERNANCE /Resources/285741-1343934891414/8787489-1344020463266/8788935 -1399321576201/RTI_Case_Studies_Implementation_WEBfinal.pdf.

Dokeniya, Anupama. 2013. *Implementing Right to Information: Lessons from Experience*. Washington, DC: World Bank. http://siteresources.worldbank.org/PUBLICSECTOR ANDGOVERNANCE/Resources/285741-1343934891414/8787489 -1344020463266/RTI-IPP-Web-Final.pdf.

———. 2014. "The Right to Information as a Tool for Community Empowerment." In *The World Bank Legal Review Volume 5: Fostering Development through Opportunity, Inclusion, and Equity*, edited by Hassan Cisse, N. R. Madhava Menon, Marie-Claire Cordonier Segger, and Vincent O. Nmehielle, 599–614. Washington, DC: World Bank. https://openknowledge.worldbank.org/bitstream/handle/10986/16240/82558 .pdf?sequence=1.

Donaldson, A., and P. Walker. 2004. "Information Governance—A View from the NHS." *International Journal of Medical Informatics* 73: 281–84.

Economist Intelligence Unit. 2008. *The Future of Enterprise Information Governance*. London: Economist Intelligence Unit.

Excell, Carole. 2011. *Implementation of a Freedom of Information Law: Top 10 Things to Do in First 6 Months*. Washington, DC: Access Initiative. http://www.accessinitiative.org /blog/2011/09/top-10-things-do-first-six-months-implement-a-freedom-information -law-one-view.

Fox, Jonathan, and Libby Haight. 2011. "Mexico's Transparency Reforms: Theory and Practice." In *Mexico's Democratic Challenges: Politics, Government, and Society*, edited by Andrew Selee and Jacqueline Peschard, 353–79. Redwood City, CA: Stanford University Press. https://ideas.repec.org/p/cdl/glinre/qt7nf8b01r.html.

Fukuda-Parr, Sakiko, Patrick Guyer, and Terra Lawson-Remer. 2011. "Does Budget Transparency Lead to Stronger Human Development Outcomes and Commitments to Economic and Social Rights?" International Budget Partnerships Working Paper 4, Social Science Research Network, Rochester, NY. http://papers.ssrn.com/abstract=2211584.

Fumega, Silvana. 2015. "Understanding Two Mechanisms for Accessing Government Information and Data around the World." http://webfoundation.org/wp-content/uploads/2015/08/UnderstandingTwoMechanismsforAccessingGovernmentInformationandData.pdf.

Fung, Archon, Hollie Russon Gilman, and Jennifer Shkabatur. 2010. *Impact Case Studies from Middle Income and Developing Countries: New Technologies*. London: Institute of Development Studies. http://www.transparency-initiative.org/wp-content/uploads/2011/05/impact_case_studies_final1.pdf.

Holsen, Sarah, and Martial Pasquier. 2012. "Insight on Oversight: The Role of Information Commissioners in the Implementation of Access to Information Policies." *Journal of Information Policy* 2: 214–41.

International Records Management Trust. 2010–2011. "Managing Records as Reliable Evidence for ICT/e-Government and Freedom of Information in East Africa." http://www.irmt.org/portfolio/managing-records-reliable-evidence-ict-e-government-freedom-information-east-africa-2010—-2011.

Ionita, Sorin, and Laura Stefan. 2014. "Implementing Right to Information: A Case Study of Romania." In *Right to Information: Case Studies on Implementation*, ed. Stephanie E. Trapnell, 235–74. Right to Information Series. Washington, DC: World Bank. http://siteresources.worldbank.org/PUBLICSECTORANDGOVERNANCE/Resources/285741-1343934891414/8787489-1344020463266/8788935-1399321576201/RTI_Case_Studies_Implementation_WEBfinal.pdf (April 11, 2015).

ISO (International Organization for Standardization). 2001. *TC 46/SC 11. ISO 15489-1 Information and Documentation. Records Management. Part 1: General*. Geneva, Switzerland. http://www.iso.org/iso/iso_catalogue/catalogue_tc/catalogue_tc_browse.htm?commid=48856.

Kim, Soonhee, and Jooho Lee. 2012. "E-Participation, Transparency, and Trust in Local Government." *Public Administration Review* 72 (6): 819–28.

Kooper, M. N., R. Maes, and E. R. Lindgreen. 2011. "A Report Was Also Published on the Governance of Information: Introducing a New Concept of Governance to Support the Management of Information." *International Journal of Information Management* 31 (3): 195–200.

Lemieux, Victoria L. 2016. "One Step Forward, Two Steps Backward? Does E-Government Make Governments in Developing Countries More Transparent and Accountable?" World Development Report Background Paper, World Bank, Washington, DC. http://pubdocs.worldbank.org/pubdocs/publicdoc/2016/1/287051452529902818/WDR16-BP-One-Step-Forward-Lemieux.pdf.

Lemieux, Victoria L., Oleg Petrov, and Roger Burks. 2014. "Good Open Data . . . by Design." *Open Data: The World Bank Data Blog*. http://blogs.worldbank.org/opendata/good-open-data-design.

Levy, Brian. 2014. *Working with the Grain: Integrating Governance and Growth in Development Strategies*. Oxford: Oxford University Press.

Lipcean, Sergiu, and Laura Stefan. 2014. "Implementing Right to Information: A Case Study of Moldova." In *Right to Information: Case Studies on Implementation*, edited by Stephanie E. Trapnell, 151–78. Right to Information Series. Washington, DC: World Bank. http://siteresources.worldbank.org/PUBLICSECTORANDGOVERNANCE/Resources/285741-1343934891414/8787489-1344020463266/8788935-1399321576201/RTI_Case_Studies_Implementation_WEBfinal.pdf (April 11, 2015).

Livingstone, Aylair. 2005. "Implementation of the Access to Information Act: The Jamaican Experience—Challenges and Successes." Paper presented at the Commonwealth Human Rights Initiative Conference, New Delhi, India, May 24–26. http://www.humanrightsinitiative.org/programs/ai/rti/implementation/general/implementation_of_ai_act_jamaican_experience.pdf.

———. 2015. "Right to Information Implementation in the Caribbean Region." Presented at the Transparency and Information Management Open Discussion Forum. https://www.kaltura.com:443/index.php/extwidget/preview/partner_id/619672/uiconf_id/28169342/entry_id/1_ibilcgcv/embed/auto?.

Meknassi, Saad Filali. 2014. "Implementing Right to Information: A Case Study of Jordan." In *Right to Information: Case Studies on Implementation*, edited by Stephanie E. Trapnell, 365–418. Right to Information Series. Washington, DC: World Bank. http://siteresources.worldbank.org/PUBLICSECTORANDGOVERNANCE/Resources/285741-1343934891414/8787489-1344020463266/8788935-1399321576201/RTI_Case_Studies_Implementation_WEBfinal.pdf.

Millar, Laura. 2003. *The Right to Information—The Right to Records: The Relationship between Record Keeping, Access to Information, and Government Accountability*. http://www.humanrightsinitiative.org/programs/ai/rti/articles/record_keeping_ai.pdf.

Mizrahi, Yemile, and Marcos Mendiburu. 2014. "Implementing Right to Information: A Case Study of Mexico." In *Right to Information: Case Studies on Implementation*, edited by Stephanie E. Trapnell, 103–50. Right to Information Series. Washington, DC: World Bank. http://siteresources.worldbank.org/PUBLICSECTORANDGOVERNANCE/Resources/285741-1343934891414/8787489-1344020463266/8788935-1399321576201/RTI_Case_Studies_Implementation_WEBfinal.pdf.

Moses, Elizabeth. 2014. "Implementing Right to Information: A Case Study of South Africa." In *Right to Information: Case Studies on Implementation*, edited by Stephanie E. Trapnell, 419–74. Right to Information Series. Washington, DC: World Bank. http://siteresources.worldbank.org/PUBLICSECTORANDGOVERNANCE/Resources/285741-1343934891414/8787489-1344020463266/8788935-1399321576201/RTI_Case_Studies_Implementation_WEBfinal.pdf.

Nicro, Somrudee, Panicha Vornpien, and Nongpal Chancharoen. 2014. "Implementing Right to Information: A Case Study of Thailand." In *Right to Information: Case Studies on Implementation*, edited by Stephanie E. Trapnell, 475–538. Right to Information Series. Washington, DC: World Bank. http://siteresources.worldbank.org/PUBLICSECTORANDGOVERNANCE/Resources/285741-1343934891414/8787489-1344020463266/8788935-1399321576201/RTI_Case_Studies_Implementation_WEBfinal.pdf.

Open Government Partnership. 2015. *Open Government Partnership Guide*. http://www.opengovguide.com/.

Pereira Chumbe, Roberto. 2014. "Implementing Right to Information: A Case Study of Peru." In *Right to Information: Case Studies on Implementation*, edited by Stephanie E. Trapnell, 179–234. Right to Information Series. Washington, DC: World Bank. http://siteresources.worldbank.org/PUBLICSECTORANDGOVERNANCE/Resources/285741-1343934891414/8787489-1344020463266/8788935-1399321576201/RTI_Case_Studies_Implementation_WEBfinal.pdf.

Stammers, Neil. 2009. *Human Rights and Social Movements*. New York: Pluto Press.

Torres, Natalia, and Luis Esquivel. 2011. "Access to Information Training Approaches for Government Officials." Center for Effective Learning Environments (CELE) and University of Palermo. http://www.palermo.edu/cele/pdf/noticias/AI-training-final.pdf.

Trapnell, Stephanie E., ed. 2014. *Right to Information: Case Studies on Implementation*. Right to Information Series. Washington, DC: World Bank. http://siteresources.worldbank.org/PUBLICSECTORANDGOVERNANCE/Resources/285741-1343934891414/8787489-1344020463266/8788935-1399321576201/RTI_Case_Studies_Implementation_WEBfinal.pdf.

Trapnell, Stephanie E., and Victoria L. Lemieux. 2014. "Right to Information: Identifying Drivers of Effectiveness in Implementation." Right to Information Working Paper Series 2. World Bank, Washington, DC. http://siteresources.worldbank.org/PUBLICSECTORANDGOVERNANCE/Resources/285741-1343934891414/8787489-1344020463266/8788935-1399321576201/RTI_Drivers_of_Effectiveness_WP2_26Nov2014.pdf.

Trebicka, Jolanda, and Gerti Shella. 2014. "Implementing Right to Information: A Case Study of Albania." In *Right to Information: Case Studies on Implementation*, edited by Stephanie E. Trapnell, 3–48. Right to Information Series. Washington, DC: World Bank. http://siteresources.worldbank.org/PUBLICSECTORANDGOVERNANCE/Resources/285741-1343934891414/8787489-1344020463266/8788935-1399321576201/RTI_Case_Studies_Implementation_WEBfinal.pdf (April 11, 2015).

Worker, Jesse, with Carole Excell. 2014. "Requests and Appeals Data in Right to Information Systems: Brazil, India, Jordan, Mexico, South Africa, Thailand, United Kingdom, and United States." Working Paper, World Bank, Washington, DC. http://siteresources.worldbank.org/PUBLICSECTORANDGOVERNANCE/Resources/285741-1343934891414/8787489-1344020463266/8788935-1399321576201/Requests_and_Appeals_RTI_Working_Paper.pdf.

World Bank. 2015. "Open Data Essentials." http://opendatatoolkit.worldbank.org/en/essentials.html.

World Bank. 2016. *World Development Report 2016: Digital Dividends*. Washington, DC: World Bank.

World Wide Web Foundation. 2015. "Open Data Barometer." London, World Wide Web Foundation. http://barometer.opendataresearch.org.

Further Reading

Calland, Richard. 2003. "Turning Right to Information Law into a Living Reality: Access to Information and the Imperative of Effective Implementation." Open Democracy Advice Centre. Cape Town, South Africa. http://www.humanrightsinitiative.org/programs/ai/rti/international/laws_papers/southafrica/Calland%20-%20Turning%20FOI%20law%20into%20living%20reality%20-%20Jan-03.pdf (April 11, 2015).

Calland, Richard, and Kristina Bentley. 2013. "The Impact and Effectiveness of Transparency and Accountability Initiatives: Freedom of Information." *Development Policy Review* 31 (S1): s69–87.

Carothers, Thomas, and Saskia Brechenmacher. 2014. *Accountability, Transparency, Participation, and Inclusion: A New Development Consensus?* Washington, DC: Carnegie Endowment for International Peace. http://carnegieendowment.org/files/new_development_consensus.pdf.

Colquhoun, Anna. 2010. *The Cost of Freedom of Information.* London: Constitution Unit, University College London. http://www.ucl.ac.uk/constitution-unit/research/foi/countries/cost-of-foi.pdf.

Dokeniya, Anupama. 2014. "Implementing Right to Information: A Case Study of Uganda." In *Right to Information: Case Studies on Implementation*, edited by Stephanie E. Trapnell, 275–316. Right to Information Series. Washington, DC: World Bank. http://siteresources.worldbank.org/PUBLICSECTORANDGOVERNANCE/Resources/285741-1343934891414/8787489-1344020463266/8788935-1399321576201/RTI Case_Studies Implementation_WEBfinal.pdf.

Dragoş, Dacian C., Bogdana Neamtţu, and Bianca V. Cobârzan. 2012. "Procedural Transparency in Rural Romania: Linking Implementation with Administrative Capacity?" *International Review of Administrative Sciences* 78 (1): 134–57.

Guerrero, Juan Pablo. 2005. "The Mexican Transparency Law: Design and Implementation Experiences." Paper presented at Effective Implementation: Preparing to Operationalise the New India Right to Information Law, New Delhi. http://www.humanrightsinitiative.org/programs/ai/rti/implementation/general/maxican_transparency_law_may05.pdf.

Hazell, Robert, Ben Worthy, and Mark Glover. 2010. *The Impact of the Freedom of Information Act on Central Government in the UK: Does FOI Work?* London: Palgrave Macmillan.

Lepheana, Mothusi. 2005. "Overview of the Implementation of the Freedom of Information Legislation in South Africa." New Delhi. http://www.humanrightsinitiative.org/programs/ai/rti/implementation/general/overview_of_foi_act_south_africa.pdf.

Neuman, Laura, and Richard Calland. 2007. "Making the Law Work: The Challenges of Implementation." In *The Right to Know: Transparency for an Open World*, edited by Ann Florini, 179–213. New York: Columbia University Press.

Shepherd, Elizabeth, Alice Stevenson, and Andrew Flinn. 2010. "Information Governance, Records Management, and Freedom of Information: A Study of Local Government Authorities in England." *Government Information Quarterly* 27 (4): 337–45.

———. 2011. "Records Management in English Local Government: The Effect of Freedom of Information." *Records Management Journal* 21 (2): 122–34.

Worthy, Ben, Jim Amos, Robert Hazell, and Gabrielle Bourke. 2011. *Town Hall Transparency? The Impact of the Freedom of Information Act on English Local Government.* London: Constitution Unit Department of Political Science, University College London. http://www.ucl.ac.uk/constitution-unit/research/foi/foi-and-local-government/town-hall-transparency.pdf.

CHAPTER 4

Operating Right to Information Systems

Section 1: Systems for Responding to Requests—Procedures, Information, and Internal Tracking

Responding to requests involves several key and interrelated activities that deal with receiving incoming requests, finding and retrieving information, and tracking responses through internal systems that feed into performance monitoring efforts.

Handling Incoming Requests

Responding to an information request is rarely straightforward, and bottlenecks can occur at several states: finding and compiling responsive information, consulting with third parties, assessing and applying exceptions, and redacting exempt information (Colquhoun 2010; Shepherd, Stevenson, and Flinn 2010).

Without proper guidance on the methods to evaluate information requests, public officials may fail to distinguish between right to information (RTI)–based requests and routine information inquiries. Requests that are treated as routine information inquiries are not subject to RTI deadlines and do not benefit from protections under law, including appeals and assistance. In other cases, the formal request process involves several levels of management, and official disclosure may require approval of the secretary-general of the ministry (Dokeniya 2014, 305–6; Ionita and Stefan 2014, 252; Lipcean and Stefan 2014, 164; Trebicka and Shella 2014, 34). This over-bureaucratization motivates public officials to treat requests unofficially, because the time and effort involved with processing an official request is overwhelming. Although this tactic may be useful in terms of efficiency of response, and there will always be an important role for informal provision of information (including for journalists), it can be abused and result in discarded requests or informal refusals that do not provide a basis for appeal. The combination of extensive informality in practices or a lack of clear distinction between normal business operations and RTI requests also leads to poor tracking of requests.

Appendix D contains an example of a flowchart for information officers in the United Kingdom, as developed by the Information Commissioner's Office. It is not applicable to all contexts because of variations in RTI laws, but it is an excellent example of straightforward guidance that can be provided to officials to execute their duties in an efficient and effective fashion.

Most countries allow electronic means of submitting formal requests (online and e-mail) but require an official form to be completed and sent by requesters. Online submission, as opposed to e-mail requests, is available in some countries, but it is not always equally available across agencies. In the case of Thailand and the United States, electronic submission of requests is developed by each agency and made available on their websites (Alexander 2014; Nicro, Vornpien, and Chancharoen 2014). In contrast, India and Mexico have a centralized portal for the submission of requests that is used for access to information for any agency in the country (see figure 4.1) (Devasher Surie and Aiyar 2014; Mizrahi and Mendiburu 2014).

Identifying and Finding Information

It can be quite difficult for individuals who are outside of government to understand its operations well enough to identify where to find information that might answer a specific question or fill a knowledge gap. For this reason, whether or not

Figure 4.1 Online RTI Portals in the United States, India, and Mexico

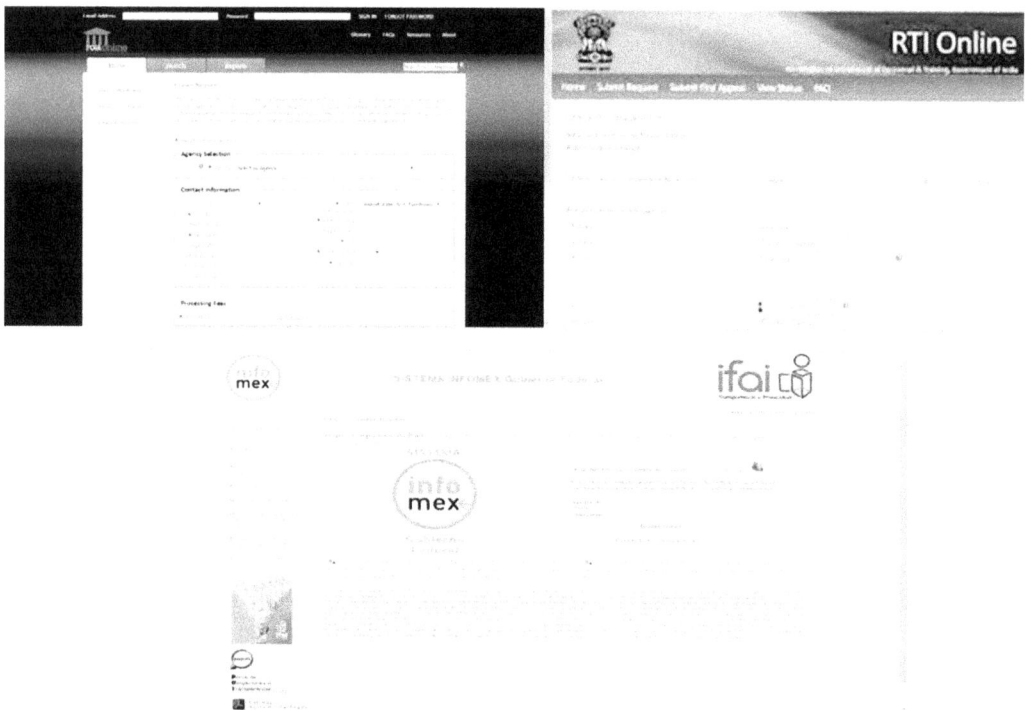

Note: RTI = right to information.

specified in the RTI law, many agencies create registers of information assets (also referred to as indexes or lists of records) to help members of the public who are unfamiliar with the structure of government find the information they are seeking. Registers may be in paper form or, increasingly, also are made available online. Publication of registers helps those making a request for access to information formulate their request more clearly, since they are able to identify and describe specific categories of records or information.

Registers benefit not only the public but also agencies. In jurisdictions where strict time limits are placed on responses to RTI requests, registers can be quite helpful since not only must the information be found, it must be found quickly. For example, when an agency receives a request for information that it does not hold, it can use registers to identify the agency that is likely to hold the information to transfer the request (see box 4.1).

Good records management is a necessary precondition for the production of registers of information. As part of managing records well, agencies will have developed (1) functional records classification schemes, which describe and support the organization and retrieval of records, and (2) retention schedules, which specify how long different categories of records should be kept and what must happen to them at the end of their retention period (e.g., destruction or transfer to a national archives). Without a good system of records management in place, the task of identifying and describing the records and information that each agency has in its custody will be made much more difficult. However, with a good record-keeping system in place, agencies will quickly be able to generate descriptions of their records and information for the production of registers that aid retrieval of information for purposes of responding to RTI requests.

Internal Tracking and Technology

Reporting data involves the tracking of responsiveness to requests and appeals processing. It is an ongoing process of collecting data on how well an RTI system is on track to meet its objectives, and it is extremely important for both real-time and end-of-year evaluations that feed into annual reporting requirements, budgets, resource allocation, and investments in technology for improved processes.

The content of internal tracking systems should include key information about the requester, departments involved in responding, and key dates of activity. Table 4.1 shows a sample of the type of information that should be considered when designing internal tracking content, whether it is manual entry in a disclosure log or through electronic tracking systems.

Online submission allows for automatic recording and tracking of requests, but country cases noted that investment in design and maintenance is required to ensure sustainability. Mexico's portal also serves as the internal tracking system for all requests and responses. This has enabled the information commission and others to identify patterns and trends in information flows that contribute to improved practices and, in particular, performance monitoring. In Thailand, the ministry of environment tracks requests for information and proactively releases

Box 4.1 Example of an Information Asset Register

The following template can be used to describe information resources.

Title: Title of resource, with additional or alternative titles if they exist.

Unique number: A unique number identifying each resource. The first part of the number may indicate which organization created the resource.

Identifier: Identifier or acronym by which the resource may be commonly known or file name with full path.

Description: A description of the information contained within the resource. An abstract if the resource is document-like. A content description of visual or other resources.

Subject: Keywords and phrases indicating the subject matter of the resource.

Coverage: Geographic area covered by the information in the resource.

Date: The date on which the resource was created or published.

Updating frequency: For databases and the like, to indicate how current the information is.

Date modified: The date on which a database or other resource was last updated.

Source: The source(s) of the information found in the resource.

Format: Physical formats of resource, such as book, CD-ROM, database (e.g., Access), collection of documents (e.g., Word, how many files).

Language: The language(s) of the resource content.

Author: Person, group, or organization responsible for the intellectual content of the resource.

Publisher: The office or organization to be contacted for further information about, or access to, the resource.

Rights: Basic indication of the user's rights to view, copy, redistribute, or republish all or part of the information held in the resource.

Category: A term or terms from the Government Category List (also called a taxonomy). Users can search for all the resources covered by each term from the list.

Source: Adapted from U.K. government, Office of Public Sector Information, *Information Asset Register*, http://tna.europarchive.org/20100402134329/http:/www.opsi.gov.uk/iar/index.

---

information with high request rates (Nicro, Vornpien, and Chancharoen 2014). Mexico has created a searchable database for all requests and responses, allowing for tracking of highly popular information and identification of information that should be proactively released (Mizrahi and Mendiburu 2014).

Section 2: Proactive Disclosure

Because of its focus on citizen uptake, proactive disclosure of information, data, and documents should be based on citizen interest, as well as agency mandate. However, very few countries have procedures to identify information for

Table 4.1 Internal Tracking Systems Content

1. Reference number	13. Date responded to requester or closed due to lack of clarification or withdrawal (dd/mm/yy)	25. How many members of staff were actively involved in responding to this request?
2. Short description		
3. Requester's name		
4. Received by	14. Working days taken to respond	26. Fee charged
5. Date received anywhere in the organization (dd/mm/yy)	15. Total time taken to respond, including inactivity (in days)	27. Exemptions applied
6. Month	16. New start date (dd/mm/yy)	28. If subject to an internal appeal, what was the outcome?
7. Type	17. Working days to go	29. If subject to an external appeal, what was the outcome?
8. Clarification sought (dd/mm/yy)	18. Extension to the deadline to allow for consideration of the public interest test	
9. Clarification received (dd/mm/yy)		30. Have you sought formal legal advice when responding to this request or appeal?
10. Request closed due to lack of clarification or withdrawal	19. Revised external date after agreed extension	
11. External due date (dd/mm/yy)	20. Outcome of public interest test	31. Has this request been subject of a review?
12. Staff deadline for supplying information (set as 10 working days before due date but can be changed) (dd/mm/yy)	21. Response	32. Review deadline
	22. Subject area	33. Review completion
	23. Type of requester	34. Review outcome
	24. Time spent actively working on the request in days	

Source: Jisc 2007/2012.

proactive disclosure beyond a standard list of categories of information to be disclosed. There is also a need for consultations with citizens and civil society organizations (CSOs) about the content of information that should be released (Darbishire 2010, 27). Information that is not relevant to users or does not meet the needs of information consumers meets only a pro forma adherence to disclosure obligations. There is a risk that, in some contexts, countries release nonsensitive information proactively to circumvent accusations of lack of efforts to implement RTI. In these cases, proactive disclosure may be seen as a passive form of resistance to information disclosure. To identify information that is most relevant to the demands of the public, agencies should at the minimum be tracking downloads or hard copy requests for proactively disclosed information.

Monitoring and oversight of proactive disclosure compliance, requests, and appeals is generally weak in all countries at present, and hence the level of compliance is uncertain. In Bangladesh, however, the cabinet division has included a provision in the performance agreements signed with line ministries specifically about proactive disclosure.[1] Tying performance on proactive disclosure into performance plans, such as Bangladesh has done, can incentivize proactive disclosure and promote greater compliance.

Comparative analysis of national legislation yields a list of the most common information that is included in proactive disclosure efforts (see box 4.2).

Specialized information and communication technology (ICT) tools are intended to streamline the process of online disclosure to keep costs down (Fumega 2014).[2] But they are often a major investment, and without

Box 4.2 Suggested List of Information to Release Proactively

- *Institutional information:* Legal basis of the institution, internal regulations, functions, and powers.
- *Organizational information:* Organizational structure including information on personnel and the names and contact information of public officials.
- *Operational information:* Strategy and plans, policies, activities, procedures, reports, and evaluations, including the evidence and other documents and data being used as a basis for formulating them.
- *Decisions and acts:* Decisions and formal acts, particularly those that directly affect the public, including the data and documents used as the basis for these decisions and acts.
- *Public services information:* Descriptions of services offered to the public, guidance, booklets and leaflets, copies of forms, information on fees and deadlines.
- *Budget information:* Projected budget, actual income and expenditure (including salary information), and other financial information and audit reports.
- *Open meetings information:* Information on meetings, including which are open meetings and how to attend these meetings.
- *Decision making and public participation:* Information on decision-making procedures including mechanisms for consultations and public participation in decision making.
- *Subsidies information:* Information on the beneficiaries of subsidies, the objectives, amounts, and implementation.
- *Public procurement information:* Detailed information on public procurement processes, criteria, and outcomes of decision making on tender applications, copies of contracts and reports on completion of contracts.
- *Lists, registers, databases:* Information on the lists, registers, and databases held by the public body. Information about whether these lists, registers, and databases are available online and/or for on-site access by members of the public.
- *Information about information held:* An index or register of documents/information held including details of information held in databases.
- *Publications information:* Information on publications issued, including whether publications are free or the price if they must be purchased.
- *Information about RTI:* Information on the right of access to information and how to request information, including contact information for the responsible person in each public body.

Source: Darbishire 2010, 29–30.
Note: RTI = right to information.

appropriate training and skilled information technology (IT) staff to deal with interoperability difficulties among information databases, these initiatives can fail. The sustainability of these tools is also at the mercy of staffing levels, unless steps are taken to ensure that institutional knowledge remains with the organization rather than the individual. Some countries have launched centralized online portals for agencies to upload proactively disclosed information (see figure 4.2), but questions of sustainability and stakeholder support persist (Brown 2014;

Heller 2014). Based on country experiences, potential good practices for proactive disclosure include the following:

- Tracking of high-volume requests and releasing popular information (Thailand)
- A "rule of three," whereby information is released if an agency anticipates that it will be requested three times (United States)
- An online repository of requests and responses (Mexico)

Each practice requires effective data tracking and RTI usage statistics gathering processes and, in the case of using online repositories, a sustainable level of IT expertise.

Also of clear, but often overlooked, importance is that users must be able to easily find information, requiring consideration of the types of web portals for release (departmental/ministerial, centralized, sectoral) and the logic of organization within websites (by type of service, policy issue, life events, or thematic areas) (Darbishire 2010, 39–40). In terms of regularly updating information, good practice models specify timelines for mandatory updating based on the type of information being released. Two important types of proactively disclosed information are *periodic*, that is, regularly produced such as budgets and annual plans, and *ad hoc*, for example, many procurement contracts or project documents. Timelines and requirements for these types of information will vary according to their release schedules and relevance to organizational mandates.

Figure 4.2 Brazil's Proactive Disclosure Portal

The accessibility of proactively disclosed information is becoming more of a concern as Internet technology is used to disseminate documents, even in areas where Internet penetration rates are quite low (see table 4.2). Online disclosure is the most common form of proactive disclosure of information across all cases and agencies, but decentralized and disorganized approaches to maintaining pro-actively disclosed information can make such information extremely difficult to find. As a means of countering this challenge, public officials put online registers of the information that is available, sometimes via a centralized website, such as in South Africa (Moses 2014).[3] Requesters then contact agencies directly for access to the information, but this approach creates another layer of work for staff, reducing the efficiency that online proactive disclosure is designed to offer.

In contexts where Internet penetration is low or there is a need to reach specific populations (e.g., those affected by a proposed land development), alter-native methods of dissemination are sometimes employed to facilitate access to proactively disclosed information. Print media and print publications are com-mon methods to disseminate information, and all agencies cited in the case stud-ies used this method of disclosure. But low literacy levels may also require radio or television transmission or local bulletin boards featuring graphical material, along with town hall or community gatherings. Agencies in Thailand have opened One-Stop Service Centers of information, staffed by knowledgeable employees who are tasked with assisting information requesters with their searches. Information and documentation are available for inspection as specified by vari-ous provisions in the law (Nicro, Vornpien, and Chancharoen 2014, 506–10).

The quality of proactively disclosed information remains another issue, with frequent reports that many datasets are unusable (Lemieux, Petrov, and Burks 2014). Poor-quality information, lack of information about data prove-nance, and weak information stewardship all present common barriers to imple-mentation of proactive disclosure provisions. Information that must be proactively

Table 4.2 Internet Access

Country	Percentage of individuals using the Internet
Albania	60
India	15
Jordan	44
Mexico	43
Moldova	49
Peru	39
Romania	50
South Africa	49
Thailand	29
Uganda	16
United Kingdom	90
United States	84

Source: ITU (International Telecommunication Union), United Nations, 2014, http://www.itu.int/en/ITU-D/statistics.

disclosed under RTI laws usually derives from the same public sector administrative systems as other information that might be requested under RTI laws. When basic records management controls are missing, particularly in digital environments, this information—whether proactively disclosed or provided in response to a request—is likely to be incomplete, difficult to locate, and challenging to authenticate.

Evidence suggests that designing controls that will produce good-quality data and information in the first place is a far better strategy; that is, it is better to arrive at good proactively disclosed information by design. Establishment of institutional structures, responsibilities, and skills is important in agencies for them to manage their data assets with a transparent, organized process for data gathering, security, quality control, and release. To effectively carry out these responsibilities, agencies need to have (or develop) clear business processes for data management as well as staff with adequate ICT skills and technical understanding of data (e.g., formats, metadata, application program interfaces, databases) (World Bank, Open Data Working Group 2015).

Data within government are similarly critical to build on established digital data sources and information management procedures where they already exist. Good existing information management practices within government can make it much easier to find data and associate metadata and documentation, identify business ownership, assess what needs to be done to release it as open data, and put processes in place that make the release of data a sustainable, business-as-usual, downstream process as part of day-to-day information management (World Bank, Open Data Working Group 2015, 16).

Designing the institutional structures, responsibilities, and skills within government to produce good-quality information means designating one entity with sufficient authority to coordinate information governance across government. It also requires ensuring that proactive disclosure policies are implemented and that there is one agency or department responsible for information management—regardless of the form of the information (i.e., paper or digital). In regard to data and information within government, good design includes a comprehensive inventory of data and information holdings, coherent information management policies and standards, consistently enforced across government, and a process for digitization of paper records with infrastructure and processes in place for sustaining long-term digital record repositories. International standards, such as those listed in Appendix E, point the way to other good practices.

Section 3: Exemptions and Their Application

RTI laws typically contain categories of information that are exempt from disclosure. As discussed in chapter 2 such provisions are intended to guide public officials in determining what and how much information can be disclosed. Exemptions tend to describe legitimate areas requiring protection against disclosure of information, such as national security, public safety, public order, protection of public health, and protection of privacy (Right2Info n.d.). Such

exemptions may be listed in the RTI law itself or in other laws passed before or
after passage of the RTI law. Examples of other laws in which exemptions to RTI
can be found include secrecy laws, codes of administrative procedure, and
archives laws. Appendix F provides a summary of the types of exemption provisions in selected countries.

In making decisions about the application of exemptions, public officials often
have to provide proof of potential harm, as in Mexico, where the law leaves the
onus of proof on the government body that denies the requested information
(Mizrahi and Mendiburu 2014, 116). Public authorities also often have to demonstrate that the potential damage done by disclosure is higher than the benefit
(to the public) of access, as in the U.K. case discussed in chapter 2 (Lipcean and
Stefan 2014, 161). In other jurisdictions, the burden of proof is on the requester.
In addition, in the RTI laws of most jurisdictions—for example, Moldova and the
United States—so-called severability clauses require that public authorities
redact portions of documents containing sensitive information to be able to
release the remaining portions.

Some countries, such as the United Kingdom, have a high number of
exemptions in their RTI laws. The U.K. act contains 23 sections exempting
various kinds of information, and since some of these sections contain more
than one exemption, the total number of exemptions is actually higher. The
Australian Freedom of Information Act contains 17 exemption clauses, the
Canadian law contains six broad exemption clauses, and the New Zealand
law includes the equivalent of 19 exemptions spread across two clauses
(Mendel 2015). Although it might be natural to think that the higher the
number of exemptions the less likely it is that government will disclose information, in practice it depends on how the exemptions are worded. A low
number of broad exemption provisions can result in the exemption of more
information than laws that rely on a higher number of specific exemptions.
Thus, in general, it is not a question of the number of provisions but of how
the exemptions are worded, with clear guidelines and exemptions that are as
specific as possible and subject to harm and public interest tests generally
supporting greater disclosure. No matter how clearly worded, however, interpretation of the law, including by oversight bodies and the courts, plays a
critical role in giving clarity to exemptions.

Table 4.3 demonstrates that countries struggle with the quality of legal
provisions governing exemptions, as indicated by relatively low scores in the
Global RTI Rating. Exemptions to disclosure obligations include indicators on
internationally accepted exemptions, the harm and public interest tests, severability clauses that allow portions of records to be released, and reasons for
refusals.

There are, however, limited ways to address the shortcomings of exemption
provisions in RTI laws. As mentioned in chapter 2, attempts can be made to
ensure that exemptions are drafted in as clear a manner as possible and, in particular that they identify the interest to be protected. Many laws refer to vague
notions when carving out an exemption for internal processes, instead of

Table 4.3 Assessment of Country Legal Frameworks Governing RTI

Country	Right to access	Scope	Request procedures	Exceptions	Appeals	Sanctions	Promotional measures	Total
Max score	6	30	30	30	30	8	16	150
Albania	4	27	11	3	18	2	4	69
India	5	25	27	26	29	5	13	130
Jordan	0	25	7	10	8	0	5	55
Mexico	6	22	25	22	26	2	16	119
Moldova	5	28	23	23	17	4	10	110
Peru	4	29	19	17	14	4	8	95
Romania	5	29	17	13	4	6	9	83
South Africa	6	25	21	25	14	6	14	111
Thailand	4	24	14	13	14	2	5	76
Uganda	6	26	23	22	11	5	5	98
United Kingdom	2	25	20	12	23	7	10	99
United States	4	18	19	16	14	4	14	89
Average	4	25	19	17	16	4	9	

Source: Access Info Europe and the Centre for Law and Democracy's Global Right to Information (RTI) Rating, 2014, http://www.rti-rating.org/country-data.

clarifying exactly what interest is being protected, which can be used to refuse access even when the intention is that the information should be open. Better practice is to define clearly the legitimate interests to be protected, for instance, free and frank exchange of advice within government that might be thwarted by premature disclosure. In other cases, for example, for national security and privacy, laws can provide nonexclusive lists of the types of interests involved, as a means of clarifying the scope of these exceptions. However, this can also be problematic because such concepts are often highly context dependent, so that an item on the list may justify a refusal to provide information in one context but not in another one. Mendel (2014) advises that it may be better to leave this sort of elaboration to policy or guidance documents rather than including it in a binding legal document.

As discussed in chapter 2, public interest overrides are central to the balancing that takes place between imperatives for openness and reasons for nondisclosure, but they can be difficult for officials to apply and they also provide for a significant degree of administrative discretion in application.[4] Some laws simply include a general rule that information should be disclosed whenever this is in the overall public interest, despite the fact that this would pose a risk of harm to a protected interest. In Colombia, a general public interest override along these lines is accompanied by absolute overrides in relation to information that exposes human rights abuses or crimes against humanity (Mendel 2014, fn 22).

In other cases, the law provides a list of the types of public interest that might justify overriding the exemptions. In South Africa, for example, exemptions may be overridden where disclosure of the information might expose illegal acts or risks to public safety or the environment (Mendel 2014, fn 23). This has the benefit of helping to clarify the scope and nature of the public interest override but the disadvantage of being limited to the overriding public interests listed. The best approach may be exemplified by Bosnia and Herzegovina, where the law combines a general public interest override with a nonexclusive list of examples of when this might be engaged (fn 24).

Over half of the countries we studied (see table 4.4) either have state secrecy laws that supersede RTI laws or have RTI laws with broad exemptions to disclosure, making it difficult for officials to determine what kinds of information can be disclosed, particularly if they will be penalized for violating exemption requirements.[5] Even when state secrecy laws do not contradict or dominate RTI laws, questions still persist about the appropriateness of some exemption policies that maintain secrecy. This pertains to both more advanced RTI systems, such as the United States, as well as struggling systems such as Jordan, Thailand, and Uganda. Where RTI exemption provisions lack clarity or fail to provide sufficient guidance, or where other laws present conflicting guidance, as discussed in chapter 2, public officials will have to apply administrative discretion. In such cases, it is common for them to err on the side of secrecy out of fear of the risk of sanctions or internal disincentives for disclosure.

Exemption provisions represent one of the most direct ways in which the design of RTI laws influences how well the law works in practice to achieve disclosure of information. RTI laws need exemption provisions to protect against harm caused by disclosure of information. At the same time, vague or poorly worded exemption provisions can prevent legitimate disclosure of information. Careful attention must be paid to how these provisions are worded in law, regulation, and related procedural guidance, as well as to how public officials are applying such provisions in practice. Even with the best efforts to word exemption provisions clearly and narrowly, and of public officials in applying such

Table 4.4 Supporting Legal Frameworks

Country	Public consultations	Whistleblower protections	Data protection/ privacy	Competing state secrets law or broad exceptions in RTI law
Albania	No	No	Yes	Yes
India	Yes	No	Yes	No
Jordan	No	No	No	Yes
Mexico	Unknown	No	Yes	No
Moldova	No	No	Yes	Yes
Peru	Yes	Yes	Yes	Yes
Romania	Yes	Yes	Yes	Yes
South Africa	Unknown	Yes	Yes	No
Thailand	No	No	Yes	Yes
Uganda	Unknown	Yes	No	Yes
United Kingdom	Yes	Yes	Yes	Yes
United States	Unknown	Yes	No	No
Prevalence	4 out of 12	6 out of 12	9 out of 12	8 out of 12

Note: RTI = right to information.

exemptions, the complex area of exemption, such as for privacy and national security, will still need to rely upon the interpretation of oversight bodies and the courts. For this reason, as we will discuss in the following section, it is important to capture good administrative data on the operation of RTI laws in general and the application of exemption provisions specifically.

Section 4: Reporting and Performance Monitoring

Data on requests and appeals allow for a better understanding of the performance of agencies, shortcomings of the legal framework, and areas for improvement. Acknowledging high-performing agencies generates positive incentives for better performance, while poor performance can be identified and addressed. Reporting of performance data by oversight bodies is also crucial to the principle of openness. Issues of accountability come to the fore when RTI performance data are not available to all interested parties (see table 4.5).

It is, however, not surprising that RTI performance data are not reported when agencies are not aware of their own reporting obligations under the RTI law or

Table 4.5 Features of Data Tracking at the Country Level

Country	Data collector for requests and appeals	Detailed agency-level data released to the public	Manner of agency-level data release	Mandatory reporting requirements	Consistent reporting by agencies
Albania	–	–	–	–	–
India	Central Information Commission	+	Central Information Commission	+	–
Jordan	Information Council	–	–	+	–
Mexico	Federal Institute for Access to Information	+	Federal Institute for Access to Information	+	+
Moldova	–	–	–	–	–
Peru	Coordination Secretariat in the Cabinet	+	Coordination Secretariat in the Cabinet	+	–
Romania	Directorate for Governmental Strategies	+	Individual agencies	+	–
South Africa	Human Rights Commission	+	Human Rights Commission	+	–
Thailand	Official Information Commission	–	–	+	?
Uganda	Parliament	–	–	+	–
United Kingdom	Ministry of Justice	+	Information Commissioner's Office	+	+
United States	Office of Information Policy	+	Individual agencies	+	+
		7/12		10/12	3/12

Source: Trapnell and Lemieux 2014.

simply do not bother to comply with them. Reporting is often not considered a priority unless a nodal agency, enforcement body, or the law requires the submission of an annual report (Trapnell and Lemieux 2014; Worker 2014). One might expect an older, more established RTI system to benefit from better performance monitoring. In fact, the length of time since the law has been passed seems to matter less than the strength of the legal provisions regarding reporting on requests and appeals (Worker 2014).

A major challenge to incorporating RTI indicators and targets into existing administrative systems is the weakness of existing performance monitoring at the agency level. Capacity building may be required to design and implement agency-wide performance monitoring systems that can accurately and efficiently collect data. Electronic submission of requests and online portals allow for real-time tracking of information requests and outcomes, which has proved to be an enormous benefit for monitoring bodies tasked with gathering requests and appeals data (Fumega and Mendiburu 2015). However, the exclusion of marginalized groups without access to, or understanding of, the Internet presents serious issues in the generalizability of data. In the absence of government resources (or mandate) to recommend policy changes, develop good practice models, and provide more training, it is unlikely that data will be collected regularly or reliably. In resource-stretched circumstances, data often are released to the public in the hope that CSOs will use the data to highlight gaps and areas of weakness, but weaknesses are unlikely to be addressed in the absence of sufficient institutional capacity to make corrections and address gaps (see box 4.3).

In terms of identifying access to information for marginalized groups, data on the profiles of requesters are exceptionally important. However, few countries collect this kind of data, with privacy concerns cited as a significant obstacle. In countries that do collect background data on requesters, such as Brazil, Chile, and Mexico, the data include age, gender, occupation, educational level, and geographical location (Fumega and Mendiburu 2014). The types of statistics that are gathered depend upon a variety of factors, including the specificity of the national legal requirements, the performance monitoring system of each agency (and possibly the records management capacity), and the ability of the oversight agency to compel agencies to collect real-time data. In addition, the number and type of agencies that are required to report data is not the same across countries (see table 4.6). Some countries may require hundreds of agencies to report, while other countries require fewer than 50 (Worker 2014).

The credibility of RTI data reports from agencies is also a constant struggle for performance monitoring purposes. Even in strong RTI systems such as in Mexico, studies have shown that figures on effectiveness are overestimated (Fox, Haight, and Palmer-Rubin 2011). Several independent studies on compliance with RTI obligations (some conducted by in-country CSOs) have demonstrated that agencies fail to meet deadlines, keep requesters informed of status requests, and provide high-quality responses (Dokeniya 2013; Global Integrity 2006; Hazell, Worthy, and Glover 2010; Open Society Justice Initiative 2006;

Box 4.3 Types of RTI Information Reported by Public Bodies

The types of information that should be collected by monitoring bodies include a variety of information about the nature of requests, background of requesters, and the request process itself:

• Request and response data, including total annual requests at national level, and responses by type
• Timeliness of response
• Requester profile information, including type of requestor (individual, business, nongovernmental organization, media, etc.)
• Most requested information types
• Exemption data, including total refusals and most-used exemptions
• Data on appeals, including total numbers, reasons for appeal, and responses
• Sanctions data, including the number of personnel or agencies receiving sanctions for failure to release information, for destroying information, or for inappropriate release of information and
• The number of complaints registered.

Source: Worker 2014.
Note: RTI = right to information.

Table 4.6 Public Availability of RTI Data in Eight Countries

Country	Volume and responses to requests	Agencies receiving most requests	Most frequently invoked exemptions	Appeals	Sanctions
Brazil	X	X	X	X	
India	Partly	X	X		X
Jordan					N/A
Mexico	X	Partly		X	
South Africa	X			X	
Thailand				X	N/A
United Kingdom	X	X	X	X	
United States	X	X	X		

Source: Authors' compilation based on Worker 2014.
Note: Although court cases are part of the public record, right to information (RTI) data are often not compiled or aggregated to determine number of cases or outcomes. Brazil and Mexico are the only countries in the sample to collect data on the type of information sought.

Raag/NCPRI 2009; Worthy et al. 2011). Compliance testing has become more common across the sample countries we studied, with an expanded role for CSOs in the monitoring of implementation and the development of more sophisticated monitoring mechanisms by enforcement agencies.

The state of data collection and reporting by oversight agencies is far from complete or standard across countries. In many cases, it is very difficult to determine whether the data collected by central agencies are comprehensive—including all of the government agencies that fall within the scope of the law—because this information is not always made available in reports or online. Although many countries make data available on the volume of national requests and the rate of responses, either in an annual report or via an online portal, data on the use of exemptions are less prevalent, as are the reasons for appeals or how they are resolved.

Data on requests and appeals provide more insight when reviewed in combination with qualitative data on agency behavior or other surveys on public awareness of RTI. Overly aggregated statistics and lack of clear definitions in reports create limitations for analysis. Oversight and monitoring bodies need to design data monitoring systems and understand the importance of data about requests and appeals to highlight noncompliance and the need for improvement. In developing such systems, oversight bodies need to ensure that they can adequately collect and collate RTI statistics.

Notes

1. Information from Laura Maria Agosta, received September 2015.

2. For a recent analysis of ICT in RTI implementation for Brazil, Mexico, and Chile, see Fumega (2014).

3. The World Bank's own data portal offers another example of this approach (see http://data.worldbank.org/).

4. For a discussion on balancing the public interest in Commonwealth contexts, see Carter and Bouris (2006).

5. It should be noted that information contained in the table is taken from our country case studies and reflects whether broad exceptions are considered to hamper access to information in practice. In some cases, the information in table 4.4 may conflict with the scores from the Global Right to Information (RTI) Rating (Access Info Europe and the Centre for Law and Democracy, http://www.rti-rating.org/country-data), indicating that although broad exemptions may exist in law, they may not be applied universally in practice.

References

Alexander, Shannon. 2014. "Implementing Right to Information: A Case Study of the United States." In *Right to Information: Case Studies on Implementation*, edited by Stephanie E. Trapnell, 539–624. Right to Information Series. Washington, DC: World Bank. http://siteresources.worldbank.org/PUBLICSECTORANDGOVERNANCE/Resources/285741-1343934891414/8787489-1344020463266/8788935-1399321576201/RTI_Case_Studies_Implementation_WEBfinal.pdf.

Brown, Greg. 2014. "Why Kenya's Open Data Portal Is Failing—And Why It Can Still Succeed." https://sunlightfoundation.com/blog/2013/09/23/why-kenyas-open-data-portal-is-failing-and-why-it-can-still-succeed.

Carter, Megan, and Andrew Bouris. 2006. *Freedom of Information: Balancing the Public Interest*. 2nd ed. London: Constitution Unit, School of Public Policy, University College London. https://www.ucl.ac.uk/spp/publications/unit-publications/134.pdf.

Colquhoun, Anna. 2010. *The Cost of Freedom of Information*. London: Constitution Unit, University College London. http://www.ucl.ac.uk/constitution-unit/research/foi /countries/cost-of-foi.pdf.

Darbishire, Helen. 2010. "Proactive Transparency: The Future of the Right to Information? A Review of Standards, Challenges, and Opportunities." Working Paper, World Bank, Washington, DC. http://siteresources.worldbank.org/WBI/Resources /213798-1259011531325/6598384-1268250334206/Darbishire_Proactive_Transparency .pdf.

Devasher Surie, Mandakini, and Yamini Aiyar. 2014. "Implementing Right to Information: A Case Study of India." In *Right to Information: Case Studies on Implementation*, edited by Stephanie E. Trapnell, 49–102. Right to Information Series. Washington, DC: World Bank. http://siteresources.worldbank.org/PUBLICSECTORANDGOVERNANCE /Resources/285741-1343934891414/8787489-1344020463266/8788935 -1399321576201/RTI_Case_Studies_Implementation_WEBfinal.pdf.

Dokeniya, Anupama. 2013. *Implementing Right to Information: Lessons from Experience*. Washington, DC: World Bank. http://siteresources.worldbank.org/PUBLICSECTOR ANDGOVERNANCE/Resources/285741-1343934891414/8787489-1344020463266 /RTI-IPP-Web-Final.pdf.

———. 2014. "The Right to Information as a Tool for Community Empowerment." In *The World Bank Legal Review Volume 5 Fostering Development through Opportunity, Inclusion, and Equity*, edited by Hassan Cisse, N. R. Madhava Menon, Marie-Claire Cordonier Segger, and Vincent O. Nmehielle, 599–614. Washington, DC: World Bank. https://openknowledge.worldbank.org/bitstream/handle/10986/16240/82558 .pdf?sequence=1.

Fox, Jonathan, Libby Haight, and Brian Palmer-Rubin. 2011. "Proporcionar transparencia? Hasta qué punto responde el gobierno mexicano a las solicitudes de información pública?" *Gestión y política pública* 20 (1): 3–61.

Fumega, Silvana. 2014. *Information & Communication Technologies and Access to Public Information Laws*. Santiago, Chile: Ediciones Consejo para la Transparencia. http://redrta.cplt.cl/_public/public/folder_attachment/a5/1a/1a8b_42ea.pdf.

Fumega, Silvana, and Marcos Mendiburu. 2015. *Use of and Compliance with Access to Public Information Laws: Experiences in Brazil, Chile, and Mexico*. Santiago, Chile: Ediciones Consejo para la Transparencia. http://redrta.cplt.cl/_public/public/folder _attachment/a9/1a/1a8f_1b22.pdf.

Global Integrity. 2006. *Global Integrity Report*. Washington, DC. https://www.globalintegrity .org/global-report/what-is-gi-report.

Hazell, Robert, Ben Worthy, and Mark Glover. 2010. *The Impact of the Freedom of Information Act on Central Government in the UK: Does FOI Work?* London: Palgrave Macmillan.

Heller, Nathaniel. 2014. "Is Open Data a Good Idea for the Open Government Partnership?" Open Society Foundations. http://tech.transparency-initiative.org/is -open-data-a-good-idea-for-the-open-government-partnership.

Ionita, Sorin, and Laura Stefan. 2014. "Implementing Right to Information: A Case Study of Romania." In *Right to Information: Case Studies on Implementation*, edited by Stephanie E. Trapnell, 235–74. Right to Information Series. Washington, DC: World Bank. http://siteresources.worldbank.org/PUBLICSECTORANDGOVERNANCE /Resources/285741-1343934891414/8787489-1344020463266/8788935 -1399321576201/RTI_Case_Studies_Implementation_WEBfinal.pdf.

Jisc. 2007/2012. "How Long Should You Keep Information For?" http://www.jiscinfonet
.ac.uk/tools/information-request-register/.

Lemieux, Victoria L., Oleg Petrov, and Roger Burks. 2014. "Good Open Data … by
Design." *Open Data: The World Bank Data Blog.* http://blogs.worldbank.org/opendata
/good-open-data-design.

Lipcean, Sergiu, and Laura Stefan. 2014. "Implementing Right to Information: A Case
Study of Moldova." In *Right to Information: Case Studies on Implementation*, edited by
Stephanie E. Trapnell, 151–78. Right to Information Series. Washington, DC: World
Bank. http://siteresources.worldbank.org/PUBLICSECTORANDGOVERNANCE
/Resources/285741-1343934891414/8787489-1344020463266/8788935
-1399321576201/RTI_Case_Studies_Implementation_WEBfinal.pdf.

Mendel, Toby. 2014. *Recent Spread of RTI Legislation.* Right to Information Series.
Washington, DC: World Bank.

———. 2015. *Designing Right to Information Laws for Effective Implementation.* Washington,
DC: World Bank. http://siteresources.worldbank.org/PUBLICSECTORAND
GOVERNANCE/Resources/285741-1343934891414/8787489-1344020463266
/8788935-1399321576201/Law_and_Implement_FINAL.pdf.

Mizrahi, Yemile, and Marcos Mendiburu. 2014. "Implementing Right to Information: A
Case Study of Mexico." In *Right to Information: Case Studies on Implementation*, edited
by Stephanie E. Trapnell, 103–50. Right to Information Series. Washington, DC: World
Bank. http://siteresources.worldbank.org/PUBLICSECTORANDGOVERNANCE/
Resources/285741-1343934891414/8787489-1344020463266/8788935
-1399321576201/RTI_Case_Studies_Implementation_WEBfinal.pdf.

Moses, Elizabeth. 2014. "Implementing Right to Information: A Case Study of South
Africa." In *Right to Information: Case Studies on Implementation*, edited by Stephanie
E. Trapnell, 419–74. Right to Information Series. Washington, DC: World Bank.
http://siteresources.worldbank.org/PUBLICSECTORANDGOVERNANCE
/Resources/285741-1343934891414/8787489-1344020463266/8788935
-1399321576201/RTI_Case_Studies_Implementation_WEBfinal.pdf.

Nicro, Somrudee, Panicha Vornpien, and Nongpal Chancharoen. 2014. "Implementing
Right to Information: A Case Study of Thailand." In *Right to Information: Case
Studies on Implementation*, edited by Stephanie E. Trapnell, 475–538. Right to
Information Series. Washington, DC: World Bank. http://siteresources.worldbank
.org/PUBLICSECTORAND GOVERNANCE/Resour ces/285741
-1343934891414/8787489-1344020463266/8788935-1399321576201/RTI
_Case_Studies_Implementation_WEBfinal.pdf.

Open Society Justice Initiative. 2006. *Transparency and Silence: A Survey of Access to
Information Laws and Practices in Fourteen Countries.* New York: Open Society
Institute. http://www.opensocietyfoundations.org/sites/default/files/transparency
_20060928.pdf.

Right2Info. n.d. "Exceptions to Access General Standards." *Good Law and Practice.*
http://www.right2info.org/exceptions-to-access/general-standards.

Raag/NCPRI (Right to Information Assessment and Analysis Group and National
Campaign for People's Right to Information). 2009. "Safeguarding the Right to
Information—Report of the People's RTI Assessment 2008." New Delhi: NCPRI.

Shepherd, Elizabeth, Alice Stevenson, and Andrew Flinn. 2010. "Information Governance,
Records Management, and Freedom of Information: A Study of Local Government
Authorities in England." *Government Information Quarterly* 27 (4): 337–45.

Trapnell, Stephanie E., and Victoria L. Lemieux. 2014. "Right to Information: Identifying Drivers of Effectiveness in Implementation." Working Paper, World Bank, Washington DC. http://siteresources.worldbank.org/PUBLICSECTORANDGOVERNANCE /Resources/285741-1343934891414/8787489-1344020463266/8788935 -1399321576201/RTI_Drivers_of_Effectiveness_WP2_26Nov2014.pdf.

Trebicka, Jolanda, and Gerti Shella. 2014. "Implementing Right to Information: A Case Study of Albania." In *Right to Information: Case Studies on Implementation*, edited by Stephanie E. Trapnell, 3–48. Right to Information Series. Washington, DC: World Bank. http://siteresources.worldbank.org/PUBLICSECTORANDGOVERNANCE /Resources/285741-1343934891414/8787489-1344020463266/8788935 -1399321576201/RTI_Case_Studies_Implementation_WEBfinal.pdf.

Worker, Jesse. 2014. "Requests and Appeals Data in Right to Information Systems: Brazil, India, Jordan, Mexico, South Africa, Thailand, United Kingdom, and United States." Working Paper, World Bank, Washington, DC. http://siteresources.worldbank.org /PUBLICSECTORANDGOVERNANCE/Resources/285741-1343934891414 /8787489-1344020463266/8788935-1399321576201/Requests_and_Appeals_RTI _Working_Paper.pdf.

World Bank, Open Data Working Group. 2015. "Open Data Readiness Assessment (ODRA) Methodology." http://opendatatoolkit.worldbank.org/docs/odra/odra_v3 _methodology-en.pdf.

Worthy, Ben, Jim Amos, Robert Hazell, and Gabrielle Bourke. 2011. *Town Hall Transparency? The Impact of the Freedom of Information Act on English Local Government*. London: Constitution Unit Department of Political Science, University College London. http://www.ucl.ac.uk/constitution-unit/research/foi/foi-and-local-government /town-hall-transparency.pdf.

Further Reading

Boyd, Phil. 2005. "Applying the Freedom of Information Act 2000 in Practice." Paper prepared for CHRI Conference, New Delhi, India. http://www.humanrightsinitiative .org/programs/ai/rti/implementation/general/uk_regulation_under_foi_act.pdf.

Dokeniya, Anupama. 2014. "Implementing Right to Information: A Case Study of Uganda." In *Right to Information: Case Studies on Implementation*, edited by Stephanie E. Trapnell, 275–316. Right to Information Series. Washington, DC: World Bank. http:// siteresources.worldbank.org/PUBLICSECTORANDGOVERNANCE/Resources /285741-1343934891414/8787489-1344020463266/8788935-1399321576201/RTI _Case_Studies_Implementation_WEBfinal.pdf.

Guerrero, Juan Pablo. 2005. "The Mexican Transparency Law: Design and Implementation Experiences." Paper presented at Effective Implementation: Preparing to Operationalise the New India Right to Information Law, New Delhi. http://www .humanrightsinitiative.org/programs/ai/rti/implementation/general/maxican _transparency_law_may05.pdf.

ISO (International Organization for Standardization). 2001. *TC 46/SC 11. ISO 15489-1 Information and Documentation. Records Management. Part 1: General*. Geneva, Switzerland. http://www.iso.org/iso/iso_catalogue/catalogue_tc/catalogue_tc_browse .htm?commid=48856 (April 16, 2015).

Kim, Soonhee, and Jooho Lee. 2012. "E-Participation, Transparency, and Trust in Local Government." *Public Administration Review* 72 (6): 819–28.

Millar, Laura. 2003. *The Right to Information—The Right to Records: The Relationship between Record Keeping, Access to Information, and Government Accountability.* http://www.humanrightsinitiative.org/programs/ai/rti/articles/record_keeping_ai.pdf.

United Kingdom Information Commissioner's Office. 2013. *The Public Interest Test: Freedom of Information Act.* London. https://ico.org.uk/media/for-organisations/documents/1183/the_public_interest_test.pdf.

United Nations OHCHR (Office of the High Commissioner for Human Rights). 2014. "The Right to Privacy in the Digital Age." United Nations, New York. http://www.ohchr.org/EN/HRBodies/HRC/RegularSessions/Session27/Documents/A.HRC.27.37_en.pdf.

CHAPTER 5

Monitoring Implementation and Evaluating Impact

Section 1: Use and Impact of RTI on Development

A growing body of literature offers evidence of the impact of a broad range of initiatives assigned the transparency label, including right to information (RTI) (Calland and Bentley 2013; Levy 2014, 160). This literature seeks to answer the question, Why does transparency (or RTI in particular) matter? Much of it draws differing conclusions about the impact of transparency on development outcomes. Some studies show very positive outcomes, whereas others suggest that transparency mechanisms, such as RTI, may have negative outcomes.

A study conducted by Daniel Berliner linking RTI laws and increased foreign direct investment (FDI) provides evidence of positive outcomes and points the way to future work that could be undertaken to better understand the contribution of RTI laws to development. Using a panel study of 72 developing countries over the years 1985 to 2008, Berliner (2012) found that those countries that have passed RTI laws received significantly more FDI than those that had not passed such laws. This proved true, however, only for countries with laws in effect for three or more years and where the strength of RTI laws in practice was higher. Berliner observes that RTI laws can increase FDI in two ways:

> They can lead to greater direct transparency, and they can increase policy credibility. [RTI] laws lead to greater transparency by increasing the quantity, quality, and accessibility of information about the business environment, domestic political actors' preferences, and the policymaking process. This information in turn reduces investor uncertainty about potential host country attributes, and increases the likelihood of advance warning in the case of future policy changes or expropriation. FOI laws can increase policy credibility by placing monitoring and sanctioning ability in the hands of a greater number of domestic actors, making future policy reversals less likely. (Berliner 2012, 142)

As anecdotal evidence of the impact of RTI laws on the business environment and FDI, Berliner cites the book *Doing Business in India for Dummies*, which includes a section entitled "Putting India's Right to Information Act to Good Use," claiming that the law has helped with "clearing Indian business hurdles," especially by speeding up regulatory delays (Berliner 2012, 147). Berliner's study is just one of many that has found RTI laws to have had a positive impact.[1]

On the other hand, various studies claim that assertions about the impact of RTI laws are overblown or even, in some respects, negative. Darch and Underwood (2010) are among those who have written that claims about the universal benefit of RTI laws have been overstated. Others suggest that RTI laws may have unintended negative consequences, such as producing increased public mistrust of government and greater unwillingness of public officials to discuss policy options openly and in a nonpartisan manner.[2] Francis Fukuyama, for example, has made the claim that the United States is in trouble because of an imbalance between the strength and competence of the state, on the one hand, and the institutions that were originally designed to constrain the state, on the other. In his latest book, Fukuyama suggests that American democracy has become dysfunctional partly because of excesses in transparency. Too much openness, he worries, has undermined the effectiveness and legitimacy of government (see Fukuyama 2014). This has led to challenges to the value of RTI and greater government openness.

One reason that these studies arrive at different conclusions about the impact of transparency on development is that they rely upon different theories of change. Another is that they measure different levels of impact (i.e., some measure first-order outcomes, whereas others focus on second- or third-order outcomes by our definition). Yet another reason is that they use different methods of analysis: Some are case studies, others offer meta-analyses, and others use statistical approaches. Another complicating factor is a lack of baseline data in the studies on the level of implementation of RTI laws that would make it possible to compare "apples with apples" rather than "apples with oranges." Thus, the current body of literature makes it very difficult to make any strong assertions about the impact of RTI.

Rather than attempt to make any definitive arguments about the broad socioeconomic impact of RTI laws, we summarize below four examples illustrating how RTI has been used successfully as a transparency transmission mechanism to achieve second- and third-degree development outcomes. We frame discussion of the examples in terms of three transmission mechanisms of transparency and, thus, of RTI: (1) "upstream" mechanisms, allowing citizens to hold politicians to better account, that is, the "voice" channel of the long route to accountability; (2) "bottom-up" mechanisms that are not aimed at supporting accountability as a whole but at specific localized gains, such as improvements in teacher attendance (in other words, the so-called short route to accountability); and (3) a mechanism that bypasses the public sector entirely and embraces parallel, participatory arrangements for service delivery (Levy 2014, 161–62). Levy suggests that all of these mechanisms may prove effective, but he also cites literature suggesting that, "for bottom-up initiatives to add value, they need to support (or be supported by) the broader framework of formal institutions. Put differently, they need to embrace the first transmission mechanism." An example of this is the way in which existing RTI laws support more effective open contracting (Cambridge Economic Associates and PDG South Africa 2014). The examples come from across a variety of sectors in countries of different income levels in which the laws have been in place for varying lengths of time and do not have the same level of quality even though their quality ratings are all above average according to the Global RTI Rating.[3]

Example 1
Sector: Food subsidies
Country: India
Income level: Lower middle
Year of RTI law passage: 2005
Global RTI Rating: 128 (ranked third overall)
Mechanism: Both upstream (in the sense of holding public officials to account for falsification of records about food subsidies) and bottom-up (in terms of improving the distribution of food subsidies).
Impact of RTI:
In India, RTI laws are regularly used by advocates for the poor to obtain records on distribution of food subsidies to show that individuals' names have been forged and records have been falsified, and to ensure the food subsidies are given to those entitled to receive them (Banisar 2011). This use of RTI laws has benefited individual recipients of food subsidies and, over time, as individual cases have been addressed, has resulted in improvements of the condition for a number of people (i.e., a second-degree outcome). Whether these improvements have had a lasting socioeconomic impact (i.e., a third-degree outcome) is still unclear, however.

Example 2
Sector: Health and safety
Country: United Kingdom
Income Level: High
Year of RTI law passage: 2000
Global RTI Rating: 99 (ranked 30th overall)
Mechanism: Upstream
Impact of RTI:
Civil society groups' support of RTI legislation was motivated by a desire to break the close relations that had developed between regulatory authorities and industry. Regulators had historically sought to preserve these close relations by, among other things, invoking the Official Secrets Act and by refusing to divulge the results of inspections to third parties (such as members of the public whose quality of life was affected by industrial pollution). The elimination of the proposed exemption covering the results of health and safety investigations (for example, product safety reports, pollution investigations,

and documents concerning workplace accidents) represented an example of civil society organizations (CSOs) using RTI to prevail over the interests of state actors working on behalf of industry rather than in the public interest (i.e., a second-degree outcome; see Trapnell 2014). Longer-term socioeconomic impact (i.e., third-degree outcome) remains difficult to ascertain.

Example 3
Sector: Environment
Country: Bangladesh
Income level: Low
Year of RTI law passage: 2008
Global RTI Rating: 107 (ranked 20th overall)
Mechanism: Bottom-up
Impact of RTI:
In 1998 the Bangladesh Garment Manufacturers and Exporters Association (BGMEA) started the construction of a new building in Hatirjheel, Dhaka. The land had been set aside for the Begunbari-Hatirjheel integrated development project, whose main objective was to drain stagnant water from the city during the rainy season. Thus, there were allegations that the BGMEA tower was the main reason for chronic and severe waterlogging in Dhaka city. After many efforts to obtain information from the Capital Development Authority of the government of Bangladesh, the requested information was handed over to the Bangladesh Environmental Lawyers Association (BELA). The collected information clearly indicated that approval for the sale of the land was given conditional upon fulfill-ment of some legal conditions, which were not followed afterwards. A report was published in the daily newspaper *The New Age* on October 2, 2010, which drew the issue to the attention of public authorities and gave it wider attention. Accordingly, a legal case started in court. This turned into a movement to ensure that proper procedures are followed and the land is used in the best interest of the people. In the court ruling, it was noted that the BGMEA did not own the land on which the building was constructed. The BGMEA building was ordered to be demolished because of this violation of the law. As per the RTI act, BELA found that the Central Development Authority had not nominated a departmental information officer (DIO), and BELA made a complaint to the Information Commission. After receiving an order from the commission, a DIO was appointed (Commonwealth Human Rights Initiative, ANSA, and World Bank Institute Access to Information Program 2011). This example demonstrates effective implementation of the law (i.e., first-order outcome), even without the appointment of a DIO in the Central Development Authority, and subsequent strengthening of implementation. It also demonstrates use of the RTI law to foment positive socioeconomic change, in the particular case of the BGMEA building, but more important in terms of the introduction of new procedures around land use (i.e., second-order outcome). In this case also it is difficult to determine the extent to which the second-order outcomes led into long-term socioeconomic improvements or third-order outcomes.

Example 4
Sector: Farm subsidies
Country: Mexico
Income level: Upper middle
Year of RTI law passage: 2002
Global RTI Rating: 117 (ranked eighth overall)
Mechanism: Bottom-up and participatory
Impact of RTI:
In 2007, the Mexican nongovernmental organization (NGO) FUNDAR requested information from the Ministry of Agriculture on recipients of PROCAMPO, the largest federal farm subsidy program in the country, designed to increase agricultural productivity, support the poorest farmers, and reduce the high levels of inequality in Mexico's rural sector. The Ministry of Agriculture responded to this information request, but the information was incomplete and delivered in non-machine-readable formats. The NGO appealed to IFAI (Instituto Federal de Acceso a la Información [Federal Institute for Access to Information]), the oversight body, which resolved in favor of the NGO and directed the Ministry of Agriculture to release the complete list of recipients and provide the documents in a machine-readable format. After obtaining the information from the Ministry of Agriculture, FUNDAR—along with other NGOs and academic institutions—launched a project called Farm Subsidy in Mexico, which systematized and ordered the information and posted it online in a searchable format. The website database allows citizens to search the list of beneficiaries of farm subsidies over the past 15 years and to compare payments and distributional patterns across states. This information confirmed that the bulk of farm subsidies had not been allocated to the country's poorest and smallest farmers, as the program originally intended, but to the wealthiest farmers in the country. Moreover, an analysis of the list of recipients revealed that beneficiaries did not always meet the recipients' selection criteria. The news intensified the pressure on the Ministry of Agriculture to revise the program's operating rules and to clean up its list of recipients. Several high-level officials resigned amid pressure for reform, and the government announced a review and reform of PROCAMPO's rules of operation. The government established a minimum of 1,300 pesos ($100) and a ceiling of 100,000 pesos ($8,000) per farmer per harvest cycle. However, the government did not introduce incentives to ensure compliance with the new PROCAMPO operating rules. Nor were sanctioning mechanisms introduced (Mizrahi and Mendiburu 2014). This example demonstrates effectiveness in implementation and operation of the RTI law (i.e., a first-order outcome), as well as evidence of second-order outcomes in the form of the introduction of new operating rules that realigned distribution of the farm subsidies. Third-order outcomes are less certain, however.

These four examples provide anecdotal evidence of the impact that RTI laws can have in a variety of sectors using a range of transmission mechanisms. What they do not provide, however, is systematic evidence of a causal link between the characteristics of RTI laws (e.g., initial quality or degree of implementation), on the one hand, and types of transmission mechanisms or downstream development outcomes, on the other. At best, it is possible only to infer from the very diversity of the cases that RTI laws can foment positive change in a variety of contexts. The cases also point to some intriguing questions about relationships between the laws and other factors that warrant further exploration: How important is the initial quality of an RTI law in determining its downstream impact? Have RTI laws been used more successfully in one sector than in others? Do particular RTI transmission mechanisms work better in some country contexts than others? How important are nonstate actors, such as CSOs or the media, in the operation of transmission mechanisms and downstream impact? Are there other factors, such as the quality of governance or level of corruption in a country, that should be considered in deciding on the use of a particular RTI transmission mechanism to achieve the greatest impact? These lines of enquiry can only be answered with more comprehensive and comparable data about the impact of RTI laws and their level of implementation, which is not currently available. Further understanding is also complicated by the fact that many intervening contextual factors make it difficult to compare across countries. It is to a discussion of addressing this data challenge that we turn in the next section.

Section 2: Monitoring the Implementation of RTI Laws

Though cases such as the ones cited in the previous section demonstrate that RTI laws can have positive effects, the challenge of measuring the impact of RTI laws on development ultimately rests upon having well-defined indicators grounded in a robust theoretical framework. Indicators that measure the effective implementation of RTI laws across countries would enable researchers to study the relationship between, on the one hand, the existence of laws, the quality of laws, and levels of implementation of the laws, and, on the other hand, measures of government openness, effective governance, citizens' perceptions of trust, the business environment, and measures of poverty and economic growth. This would provide a foundation for gaining a better understanding not only of what particular components of RTI implementation are most important for driving effective RTI implementation, but also of how effective RTI implementation drives effective governance and broader development outcomes.

At present, however, there is no one single global set of such indicators. Instead, currently a range of indicators are available for different aspects of open and transparent government produced by multilateral agencies and CSOs (see box 5.1). These indicators cover different sets of countries, examine different spheres of government transparency, and use a variety of criteria and methodologies. Some focus, for example, on specific types of information or sectors, such as the openness of government budgets or the availability of information within the extractive industries. Others are broader in scope and provide measures of access to information or transparency in general. In spite of their limitations in scope and methodology, such indicators can be useful as analytical tools to identify areas needing reform. In addition, they can activate citizen engagement when used as a means of generating discussion.

Box 5.1 Openness and Transparency Indicators

World Bank indicators

- Worldwide Governance Indicators
- Public Accountability Mechanisms
- Country Policy and Institutional Assessment (CPIA) transparency, accountability, and corruption in the public sector rating

Other indicators and assessment tools

- Africa Integrity Indicators (https://www.globalintegrity.org/initiative/africa-integrity/)
- Afrobarometer (http://www.afrobarometer.org/)
- Aid Transparency Index (http://ati.publishwhatyoufund.org/)
- Assessment of Access to Information in Latin American Countries (Spanish)
- Carter Center Implementation Assessment Tool
- Centre for Law and Democracy Global RTI Rating
- Gateway Corruption Assessment Toolbox
- Global Integrity Index
- Government of Catelonia Indicators for evaluation of transparency
- Index of Right to Information Laws in Mexico (Spanish)
- International Budget Partnership (http://internationalbudget.org/what-we-do/open-budget-survey/)
- International Institute for Democracy and Electoral Assistance (IDEA) State of Democracy Assessment Framework
- Justice Initiative Access to Information Monitoring Tool: Report from a Five-Country Pilot Study
- Open Data Barometer
- Open Democracy Advice Centre Golden Key Awards
- Open Government Portfolio Public Value Assessment Tool (http://www.ctg.albany.edu/publications/online/pvat)
- Organisation for Economic Co-operation and Development (OECD) Open Government Survey
- Public Financial Management Performance Measurement Framework (http://www.pefa.org/en/content/pefa-framework-material-1)
- QuODA (http://www.cgdev.org/page/quality-oda-quoda)
- Resource Governance Index (http://www.resourcegovernance.org/rgi)
- Sustainable Governance Indicators (http://www.sgi-network.org)
- Transparency International Corruption Perception Index
- The Web Index (http://thewebindex.org).

Source: Coronel 2012.
Note: RTI = right to information.

To assess the effectiveness of RTI implementation in a particular context as well as to develop a robust theoretical understanding of RTI in relation to development outcomes, RTI-specific indicators are needed.

Various indicators measure aspects of RTI laws. In general, these can be grouped into two basic categories: de jure and de facto measures. De jure indicators measure several aspects of the laws, such as categories of provisions (e.g., scope, oversight, accessibility) or their overall quality, whereas de facto measures focus on the manner in which the laws are functioning in practice. Although de jure measures are useful, they do not say much about the effectiveness of the laws. Thus, ultimately, to understand the impact of RTI laws on governance or development, it is necessary to have de facto indicators.

De facto indicators can be grouped into three broad categories (see figure 5.1):

1. *Input-oriented indicators:* These examine whether a particular component that is necessary for the operation of an RTI regime, for example, the appointment of public information officers or the establishment of records management systems, is in place. However, such indicators, though useful, tend not to provide insights into how the laws are operating in practice. For this, output-oriented indicators are needed.
2. *Output-oriented indicators:* These types of indicators measure operational features of RTI laws, such as how many requests are received, how many are responded to and in what time frame, what percentage of the requests resulted in disclosure of information, amount of data proactively disclosed, and so on. These types of indicators, too, have their limitations if the intent is to measure

Figure 5.1 Types of De Facto RTI Indicators

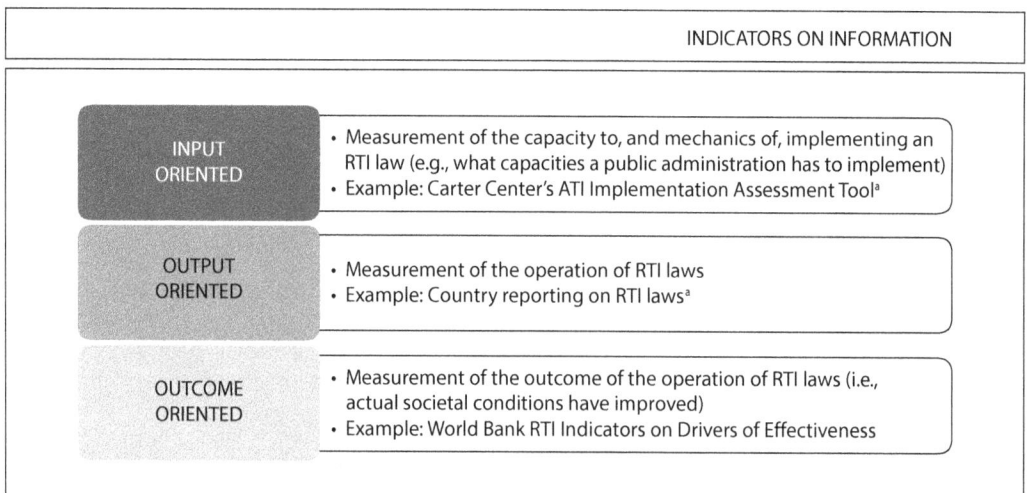

Source: Lemieux 2015.
Note: ATI = access to information; RTI = right to information.
a. Scope of measurement may be at the country level or at the level of public bodies/agencies.

the effect of RTI laws on governance and development outcomes. For one thing, such measures do not reveal whether information, even if disclosed, was used to bring about positive change. In addition, the data available on output-oriented indicators are often derived from poor-quality administrative systems or have been created by civil society groups from available sources and, thus, are often of very poor quality (Worker with Excell 2014).

3. *Outcome-oriented indicators:* These are the most difficult measures to develop, but arguably the most revealing. They measure the effectiveness of RTI laws in terms of their impact. As mentioned in chapter 1, the results chain from establishment of an RTI law, and its operation, to poverty reduction and economic development, for example, is long and difficult to measure. It is therefore more realistic, and likely more accurate, to begin by thinking of outcomes in terms of degrees of impact (e.g., first, second, and third), as we have previously proposed.

Outcome indicators for the first two categories above can be subdivided into two categories: those that are direct measures of the outcomes of effective RTI laws and those that measure the drivers of effective outcomes. The former measures what *is* occurring, and the latter predicts what the outcome *will be*. Of the direct measures of outcome, measures exist that are experience-based, such as those that submit test requests for information related to a particular sector, service, or group in society (e.g., women) to determine how well the system operates in responding to such requests. There are also measures of perception, that is, of whether people in a society believe that information is more freely available to them because they have a legal RTI. The second category of outcome-oriented indicators comprises those that measure drivers of effective RTI implementation to predict upstream what will be the likelihood of successful downstream development outcomes. The World Bank RTI Indicators on Drivers of Effectiveness fit into this latter category (see box 5.2). A description of the main components of the indicators is given in appendix B.

How do we know that these indicators will be good predictors of first-degree RTI effectiveness? Most indicators have been developed by means of a consensus-building process among key members of an epistemic community. Unlike these indicators, the RIDE indicators derive from a thematic synthesis of a series of structured case studies analyzed using a grounded-theory-based qualitative research methodology that was checked for intercoder reliability.[4] As with any methodological approach, several limitations to this work can be cited. The data collection and frame for analysis for the underlying case studies were structured by a set of parameters (or indicators) that were informed by prior research and practitioner expertise. In addition, the case studies that serve as the basis for the indicators were researched and written by a variety of authors, with different levels of focus and knowledge, but with extensive experience in studying or working with RTI systems. They brought different skill sets to the analysis and applied their own specific understandings of what matters for RTI systems to the subject matter, albeit within an analytical framework that required triangulation

Box 5.2 Goals of RTI Indicators on Drivers of Effectiveness

In an attempt to encompass a wider frame of study than responsiveness, performance, or the mechanics of implementation, the RTI Implementation: Drivers of Effectiveness (RIDE) indicators focus on the precursors to implementation effectiveness, that is, what is preventing or facilitating implementation in practice. This is not a question of whether specific outcomes are achieved, but rather, an inquiry into the drivers of implementation that lead to effectiveness. With this frame, it is important to capture the relevance of specific spheres of work on RTI implementation. The domains of RTI implementation and their related drivers of effectiveness, as presented throughout this guide, provide the theoretical structure upon which the indicators are built.

These indicators are intended to identify problem areas, so-called red flags, as well as areas of success, using the most objective data available. Data are collected through evidence-based expert assessment, where two forms of supporting documentation are required for each indicator score, and a peer review process is used for quality control and reliability purposes.

The RIDE indicators should not be considered a systematic, in-depth assessment of an RTI system. This is particularly true because of in-country variation in the performance of public bodies. There is thus a need for more focused examination, which cannot be achieved with a national-level evidence-based expert assessment study.

of data for reliability purposes. As a further future reliability check, measures of RTI effectiveness based on the RIDE indicators can be triangulated with other direct measures of RTI outcomes.

The indicators were pilot tested in six countries and found to work effectively as a tool to gather data on key aspects of RTI regimes responsible for driving effectiveness. The six countries studied were Albania, Jordan, Scotland, South Africa, Thailand, and Uganda. Five of the countries were studied previously in the volume of case studies examining RTI implementation, published in 2014 by the World Bank, and serving as the basis for the subsequent synthesis report (Trapnell 2014). Country findings from the pilot study correlated strongly with the conclusions in the RTI country case studies (see box 5.3).

Based on the nature of the indicators and current findings, the data can be used by a variety of stakeholder groups. This includes using the data (1) as a basis for stakeholder consultations and/or collaboration as well as advocacy points for civil society, (2) as inputs for policy-relevant action for governments, (3) to monitor progress on levels of implementation of RTI laws (e.g., in the context of development projects or the United Nations' Sustainable Development Goals), and (4) for statistical analysis of correlations to enhance the theoretical underpinnings of RTI policy.

Box 5.3 Key Findings from the Pilot Study of the RIDE Indicators

Key findings from the pilot study include the following:

- Demand for information emerged as a weak point for nearly all the countries surveyed, with *very weak* to *moderate* scores reported for the accessibility indicators.
- Records management scored poorly across the entire range of countries, suggesting that this area is an overlooked and weakly functioning foundation for RTI implementation.
- Staff knowledge indicators scored very poorly, despite moderately high scores on training and availability of guidance materials to staff.
- Countries are failing to set appropriate job demands, clear rules, clear lines of accountability, and strong career prospects for officials responsible for RTI implementation on the front lines.
- Although most countries have made concerted efforts to establish stakeholder consultations, and even hold collaborative activities in training and public outreach, a profound lack of access to decision making is still found.

Note: RIDE = RTI Implementation: Drivers of Effectiveness; RTI = right to information.

Notes

1. For a discussion of other impact assessments see Calland and Bentley (2013).
2. See, for example, Sharma (2014). As noted earlier, Sharma argues that use of the RTI laws in India has led to greater public mistrust of government and damaged democracy in India, and another author, Jason Grumet, argues that American government "is more open, more transparent, and less functional than ever before" (see Grumet, Dole, and Daschle 2014).
3. For methodology of the Global RTI Ratings, see Access Info Europe and the Centre for Law and Democracy, http://www.rti-rating.org/methodology.
4. The full methodological approach is discussed in Trapnell and Lemieux (2014).

References

Banisar, David. 2011. *The Right to Information and Privacy: Balancing Rights and Managing Conflicts.* Washington, DC: World Bank. https://www.ip-rs.si/fileadmin /user_upload/Pdf/Publikacije_ostalih_pooblascencev/Right_to_Information_and _Privacy__banisar.pdf.

Berliner, Daniel. 2012. "Institutionalizing Transparency: The Global Spread of Freedom of Information in Law and Practice." Unpublished dissertation, University of Washington. https://digital.lib.washington.edu/researchworks/handle/1773/21770.

Calland, Richard, and Kristina Bentley. 2013. "The Impact and Effectiveness of Transparency and Accountability Initiatives: Freedom of Information." *Development Policy Review* 31 (S1): s69–87.

Cambridge Economic Associates and PDG South Africa. 2014. *Disclosure of Information in Public Private Partnerships*. Washington, DC: World Bank Institute.

Commonwealth Human Rights Initiative, the ANSA (Affiliated Network for Social Accountability—South Asia), and the World Bank Institute Access to Information Program. 2011. *The Power of Using the Right to Information Act in Bangladesh: Experiences from the Ground*. Washington, DC: World Bank Institute.

Coronel, Sheila S. 2012. "Measuring Openness: A Survey of Transparency Ratings and the Prospects for a Global Index." *Freedom Info.* http://www.freedominfo.org/2012/10/measuring-openness-a-survey-of-transparency-ratings-and-the-prospects-for-a-global-index.

Darch, C., and P. G. Underwood. 2010. *Freedom of Information in the Developing World: Demand, Compliance and Democratic Behaviours*. Oxfordshire: Chandos.

Fukuyama, Francis. 2014. *Political Order and Political Decay: From the Industrial Revolution to the Globalization of Democracy*. New York: Farrar, Straus and Giroux.

Grumet, Jason, Senator Bob Dole, and Senator Tom Daschle. 2014. *City of Rivals: Restoring the Glorious Mess of American Democracy*. Guilford, CT: Lyons Press.

Lemieux, Victoria. 2015. "Indicators on Information." Presentation to United Nations, Permanent Mission of the Federal Republic of Germany and Article 19, United Nations Headquarters, New York.

Levy, Brian. 2014. *Working with the Grain: Integrating Governance and Growth in Development Strategies*. New York: Oxford University Press.

Mizrahi, Yemile, and Marcos Mendiburu. 2014. "Implementing Right to Information: A Case Study of Mexico." In *Right to Information: Case Studies on Implementation*, edited by Stephanie E. Trapnell, 103–50. Right to Information Series. Washington, DC: World Bank. http://siteresources.worldbank.org/PUBLICSECTORANDGOVERNANCE/Resources/285741-1343934891414/8787489-1344020463266/8788935-1399321576201/RTI_Case_Studies_Implementation_WEBfinal.pdf.

Sharma, Prashant. 2014. *Democracy and Transparency in the Indian State: The Making of the Right to Information Act*. Routledge/Edinburgh South Asian Studies Series. New York: Routledge.

Trapnell, Stephanie E., ed. 2014. *Right to Information: Case Studies on Implementation*. Right to Information Series. Washington, DC: World Bank. http://siteresources.worldbank.org/PUBLICSECTORANDGOVERNANCE/Resources/285741-1343934891414/8787489-1344020463266/8788935-1399321576201/RTI_Case_Studies_Implementation_WEBfinal.pdf.

Trapnell, Stephanie E., and Victoria L. Lemieux. 2014. "Right to Information: Identifying Drivers of Effectiveness in Implementation." Working Paper, World Bank, Washington, DC. http://siteresources.worldbank.org/PUBLICSECTORANDGOVERNANCE/Resources/285741-1343934891414/8787489-1344020463266/8788935-1399321576201/RTI_Drivers_of_Effectiveness_WP2_26Nov2014.pdf.

Worker, Jesse, with Carole Excell. 2014. "Requests and Appeals Data in Right to Information Systems: Brazil, India, Jordan, Mexico, South Africa, Thailand, United Kingdom, and United States." Working Paper, World Bank, Washington, DC. http://siteresources.worldbank.org/PUBLICSECTORANDGOVERNANCE/Resources/285741-1343934891414/8787489-1344020463266/8788935-1399321576201/Requests_and_Appeals_RTI_Working_Paper.pdf.

Further Reading

Carothers, Thomas, and Saskia Brechenmacher. 2014. *Accountability, Transparency, Participation, and Inclusion: A New Development Consensus?* Washington, DC: Carnegie Endowment for International Peace. http://carnegieendowment.org/files /new_development_consensus.pdf.

Cobain, Ian. 2011. "Mixed Results since Blair's 'Dangerous' Freedom of Information Act Launched." *The Guardian,* September 20. http://www.theguardian.com/politics/2011 /sep/20/mixed-results-blairs-dangerous-act.

Fox, Jonathan. 2014. "Social Accountability: What Does the Evidence Really Say?" Paper presented at the Global Partnership for Social Accountability, World Bank. http:// democracyspotdotnet.files.wordpress.com/2014/05/fox_social_accountability _evidence_gpsa_logo.pdf.

Fukuda-Parr, Sakiko, Patrick Guyer, and Terra Lawson-Remer. 2011. "Does Budget Transparency Lead to Stronger Human Development Outcomes and Commitments to Economic and Social Rights?" International Budget Partnerships Working Paper 4, Social Science Research Network, Rochester, NY. http://papers.ssrn.com/abstract =2211584.

Fung, Archon, Hollie Russon Gilman, and Jennifer Shkabatur. 2010. *Impact Case Studies from Middle Income and Developing Countries: New Technologies.* London: Institute of Development Studies. http://www.transparency-initiative.org/wp-content/uploads /2011/05/impact_case_studies_final1.pdf.

Hazell, Robert, Ben Worthy, and Mark Glover. 2010. *The Impact of the Freedom of Information Act on Central Government in the UK: Does FOI Work?* London: Palgrave Macmillan.

Peixoto, Tiago. 2013. "Does Transparency Lead to Trust? Some Evidence on the Subject." *DemocracySpot.* http://democracyspot.net/2013/06/19/does-transparency-lead-to -trust-some-evidence-on-the-subject.

Pinto, Juliet G. 2009. "Transparency Policy Initiatives in Latin America: Understanding Policy Outcomes from an Institutional Perspective." *Communication Law and Policy* 14 (1): 41–71.

Sørensen, Eva, and Jacob Torfing. 2012. "Collaborative Innovation in the Public Sector." *The Innovation Journal* 17 (1): 15–33.

Worthy, Ben, Jim Amos, Robert Hazell, and Gabrielle Bourke. 2011. *Town Hall Transparency? The Impact of the Freedom of Information Act on English Local Government.* London: Constitution Unit Department of Political Science, University College London. http://www.ucl.ac.uk/constitution-unit/research/foi/foi-and-local-government /town-hall-transparency.pdf.

CHAPTER 6

Conclusion

Passage of a right to information (RTI) law is a major achievement, and one now accomplished in more than 100 countries worldwide. Yet simply passing RTI laws is not enough to achieve more transparent, accountable, and inclusive governance and long-term development outcomes. With passage of an RTI law comes the most difficult part of realizing these outcomes: implementation. All countries face implementation challenges. Indeed, implementation is not a one-stop destination, but an ongoing process with many destinations along the way. This underscores the importance of gaining a clear picture of what drives effective implementation and how it can be achieved.

As discussed in this guide, the nature of the drivers of effectiveness and challenges to effective implementation varies by country, but, in general, a strong legal framework is a good starting point. Beyond that, enabling conditions within a country, strong demand for access to information, institutional capacity for implementation of RTI, and strong monitoring and independent oversight are all important drivers of effective implementation of RTI laws. In addition, state-society collaboration, technology, and intragovernmental collaboration may serve as amplifiers or accelerators of RTI implementation.

Of all the domains of RTI implementation, institutional capacity is possibly the most important, though good empirical evidence to make a strong assertion about this is still lacking. Without the mechanisms for disclosure, information will not be released effectively. Without functioning operations, demand falls, and there is little need for oversight. That being said, institutional capacity will not function effectively or sustainably without enabling conditions, demand for information, and oversight. All these components function together as a system for disclosure of information. The best approach is thus to institutionalize RTI within the public sector as a set of mutually reinforcing components of a system. Once institutionalized in this way, when political support wanes or oversight capacity deteriorates, the impetus to continue disclosing information will remain, even if weakened, because demand for access to information serves as a driving force to ensure sustainability and collaboration. Each component works with and reinforces the others.

How can countries advance toward more effective implementation of RTI laws? International pressure for more effective RTI implementation goes only so far. Although development of RTI laws has come about with the encouragement, assistance, or even sometimes the insistence of the international community, implementation is a less straightforward task, with many interlocking parts, and a need for sustained commitment that can be misaligned with ad hoc international support. As a result, the drive for effective implementation must come from within countries. A national coordinating strategy may therefore be a valuable tool to aid implementation, because it can serve as a guiding document when deciding on national and foreign funding priorities.

Even though the major impetus for effective implementation of RTI laws must come from within countries themselves, they need not face the challenge alone. There are, for example, international platforms that can support them in their efforts to implement RTI laws. The Open Government Partnership (OGP)[1] is a multilateral initiative that aims to secure concrete commitments from governments to promote transparency, empower citizens, fight corruption, and harness new technologies to strengthen governance. It offers an excellent opportunity for governments that qualify for membership to identify important RTI and transparency gaps and transform commitments into national action. The Global Partnership for Social Accountability (GPSA)[2] supports civil society and governments to work together to solve critical governance challenges in developing countries. The aim is to create an enabling environment in which citizen feedback is used to solve fundamental problems in service delivery and to strengthen the performance of public institutions. Once national coordinating strategies for RTI and transparency have been devised, GPSA provides opportunities for targeted support of social accountability initiatives.

An important point to remember, and a fitting point to end on, is that even when implementation is not ideal, positive impact can still be achieved. Effective implementation is, therefore, as much a journey as a destination, and one requiring sustained effort and commitment by governments, civil society, and the international community working in collaboration over the long term.

Notes

1. http://www.opengovpartnership.org/.
2. http://www.thegpsa.org/sa/.

Publications by Scottish and U.K. Information Commissioners Concerning Sequencing of Right to Information Law Implementation Activities

1. Scottish Information Commission (2004), Annual Report 2004: Summary of Implementation Activities, the first annual report produced by the Information Commissioner, covers all of the commission's work on implementation.
2. Scottish Information Commissioner (2004), Operational Plan 2004/05, organization-wide work program for the forthcoming year.
3. Scottish Information Commissioner (2004), Compliance Checklist—"Is Your Department Ready to Implement the FOI Act?"
4. Scottish Information Commissioner (2004), Preparing for Implementation: Survey of Scottish Public Authorities to Assess Their Preparedness to Implement the FOI Act (includes questionnaire).
5. Scottish Information Commissioner (2004), Preparing for Implementation: Results of Survey of Scottish Public Authorities to Assess Their Preparedness and Summary of Results.
6. U.K. Department of Constitutional Affairs (2004), Model Action Plan for Preparation for Implementation of the FOI Act.
7. U.K. National Audit Office (undated), Counting Down: Moving from Need to Know to Right to Know—Good Practice Guide on Preparing to Implement the FOIA 2000.
8. U.K. Department of Constitutional Affairs (2004), Executive Summary of Project Plan for Implementation of the FOIA 2000.
9. U.K. Department of Constitutional Affairs (undated), The Lord Chancellor's Advisory Group on Implementation of the FOIA 2000.

10. U.K. Information Rights Division (2004), Implementation of the Freedom of Information Act: High Level Project Initiation Document.

11. U.K. Department of Constitutional Affairs (undated), Role of the Information Commissioner and Department for Constitutional Affairs in Implementing the FOIA 2000.

RTI Indicators on the Drivers of Effectiveness

Table B.1 RTI Indicators on the Drivers of Effectiveness

Indicator	Description	Potential sources of data
1. Enabling conditions		
a Legal framework for RTI	Quality of legal framework assessed against international standards	Centre for Law and Democracy Global RTI Rating
b Advocacy efforts	Extent and nature of roles that civil society plays in the shaping of RTI laws and policies	CIVICUS Civil Society Index, Bertelsmann Transformation Index, interviews with CSOs
c Policy prioritization	Strength of the signaling mechanisms from government that set RTI as a critical policy initiative	Interviews with government officials, media articles, executive orders, decrees, initiatives
2. Demand for information		
a Public awareness of RTI	Extent of citizen knowledge about RTI as a right and as a set of procedures for access to information	Survey data, interviews with CSOs
b Accessibility	Accessibility of request and appeals process and proactively disclosed information	Evidence of accessibility and complaints resolution, interviews with government officials and CSOs
3. Institutional capacity		
a Updated, formal practices	Existence of practices (not rules) that public officials engage request processing, proactive disclosure, and records management	Interviews with government officials, evidence of formal practices
b Staffing levels	Assessment of whether the number of staff is sufficient to cope with RTI obligations, and how this number is arrived at	Interviews with government officials, evidence of formal practices
c Staff capacity	The knowledge of staff about RTI, and the resources at their disposal for meeting those obligations	Interviews with government officials, evidence of formal practices

table continues next page

Table B.1 RTI Indicators on the Drivers of Effectiveness *(continued)*

Indicator	Description	Potential sources of data
d	Staff incentives	Nature of the incentive structure governing the behavior of staff and management with regard to RTI	Interviews with government officials, evidence of formal practices
4. Oversight		
a	Monitoring of institutional capacity	Extent and nature of activities that support RTI implementation across government	Interviews with government officials and CSOs, aggregated performance monitoring data, compliance testing
b	Enforcement of disclosure obligations	Strength and nature of methods used to enforce RTI obligations	Interviews with government officials and CSOs, appeals and resolution data
5. Transformative factors		
a	State-society collaboration	Extent of opportunities for civil society to engage with government to jointly contribute to RTI implementation	Interviews with government officials and CSOs, evidence of meetings, workshops, strategic plans
b	Technology	Types and extent of technology used in RTI implementation	Interviews with government officials and CSOs, evidence of formal practices
c	Intragovernmental collaboration	Extent of collaboration between records management, RTI management, and technology specialists	Interviews with government officials, evidence of meetings, workshops, strategic plans

Note: CSO = civil society organization; RTI = right to information.

Institutional Arrangements for Various RTI Monitoring Tasks

Table C.1 Institutional Arrangements for Various RTI Monitoring Tasks

Country	Issuance of implementing rules	Performance monitoring	Training provision/ Training oversight	Public outreach	Issuance of best practice models/guidance	Publishing recommendations to policy makers
Albania	n.a.	n.a.	Training Institute for Public Administration	n.a.	n.a.	n.a.
India	Central and state governments	Department of Personnel and Training	Central and state governments, Institute of Secretariat and Management	Department of Personnel and Training	Department of Personnel and Training	n.a.
Jordan	n.a.	n.a.	n.a.	n.a.	n.a.	n.a.
Mexico	Federal Institute for Access to Information, Ministry of Public Administration	IFAI	IFAI, SFP	IFAI	IFAI, SFP	IFAI
Moldova	n.a.	n.a.	n.a.	n.a.	n.a.	n.a.
Peru	Public Administration Secretariat in the Office of the President of the Ministerial Cabinet	?	Public Administration Secretariat, Office of Public Defender (Ombudsman)	Office of Public Defender (Ombudsman)	?	Office of Public Defender (Ombudsman)
Romania	Ministry of Public Information (no longer exists)	n.a.	n.a.	n.a.	n.a.	n.a.
South Africa	n.a.	Human Rights Commission, Public Service Commission, Department of Justice and Constitutional Development	Human Rights Commission, Department of Justice College	Human Rights Commission	Human Rights Commission	n.a.
Thailand	Official Information Commission	n.a.	Official Information Commission	n.a.	n.a.	Official Information Commission

table continues next page

Table C.1 Institutional Arrangements for Various RTI Monitoring Tasks *(continued)*

Country	Issuance of implementing rules	Performance monitoring	Training provision/ Training oversight	Public outreach	Issuance of best practice models/guidance	Publishing recommendations to policy makers
Uganda	n.a.	n.a.	n.a.	n.a.	n.a.	n.a.
United Kingdom	Ministry of Justice	Ministry of Justice	Information Commissioner's Office, Individual agencies	n.a.	Ministry of Justice, Information Commissioner's Office	Ministry of Justice
United States	n.a.	Office of Information Policy in the Department of Justice	Office of Information Policy, individual agencies	n.a.	Office of Information Policy in the Department of Justice	Office of Government Information Services
	6/12	5/12	8/12	4/12	5/12	5/12

Note: IFAI = Instituto Federal de Acceso a la Información; n.a. = not applicable; RTI = right to information; SFP = Secretaría de la Función Pública.

Flowchart of Handling Information Requests (United Kingdom)

Start here

ico.
Information Commissioner's Office

Is it a valid request for information under FOIA? — N → Advise the requester how to make a request.

Y

Should it be dealt with as an FOI request? — N → Environmental information regulations

Data protection subject access

Normal course of business

Y

Do you wish to refuse as a vexatious or repeated request?

Have you already advised the requester that you will not respond to further vexatious/repeated requests? — N → Issue a refusal notice explaining this decision.

Y → No obligation to respond.

Y

N

Can you identify what information is being requested?

Obtain clarification from the requester.

Y

N

GO TO NEXT PAGE
Do you hold the requested information?

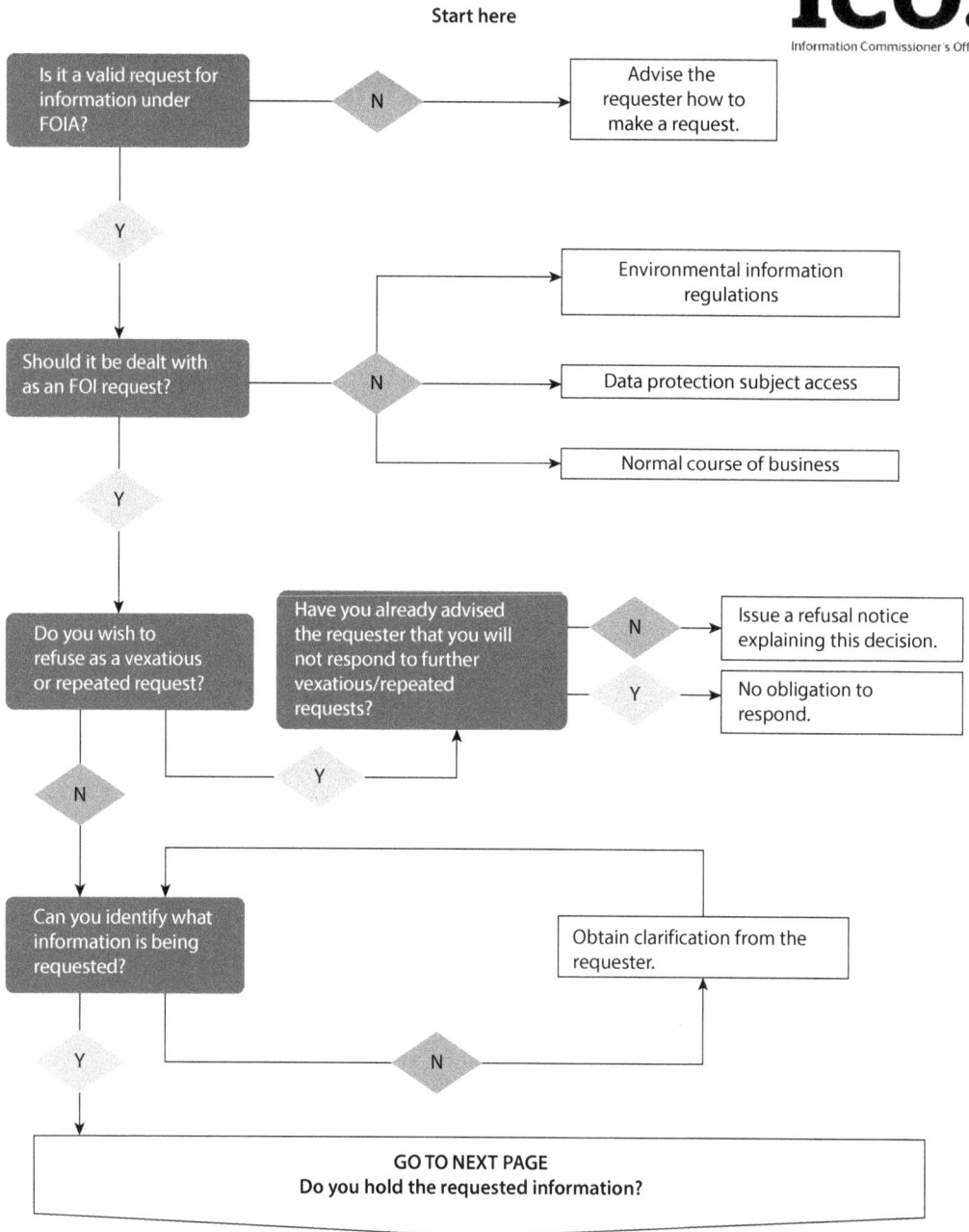

27 November 2012 v1.0

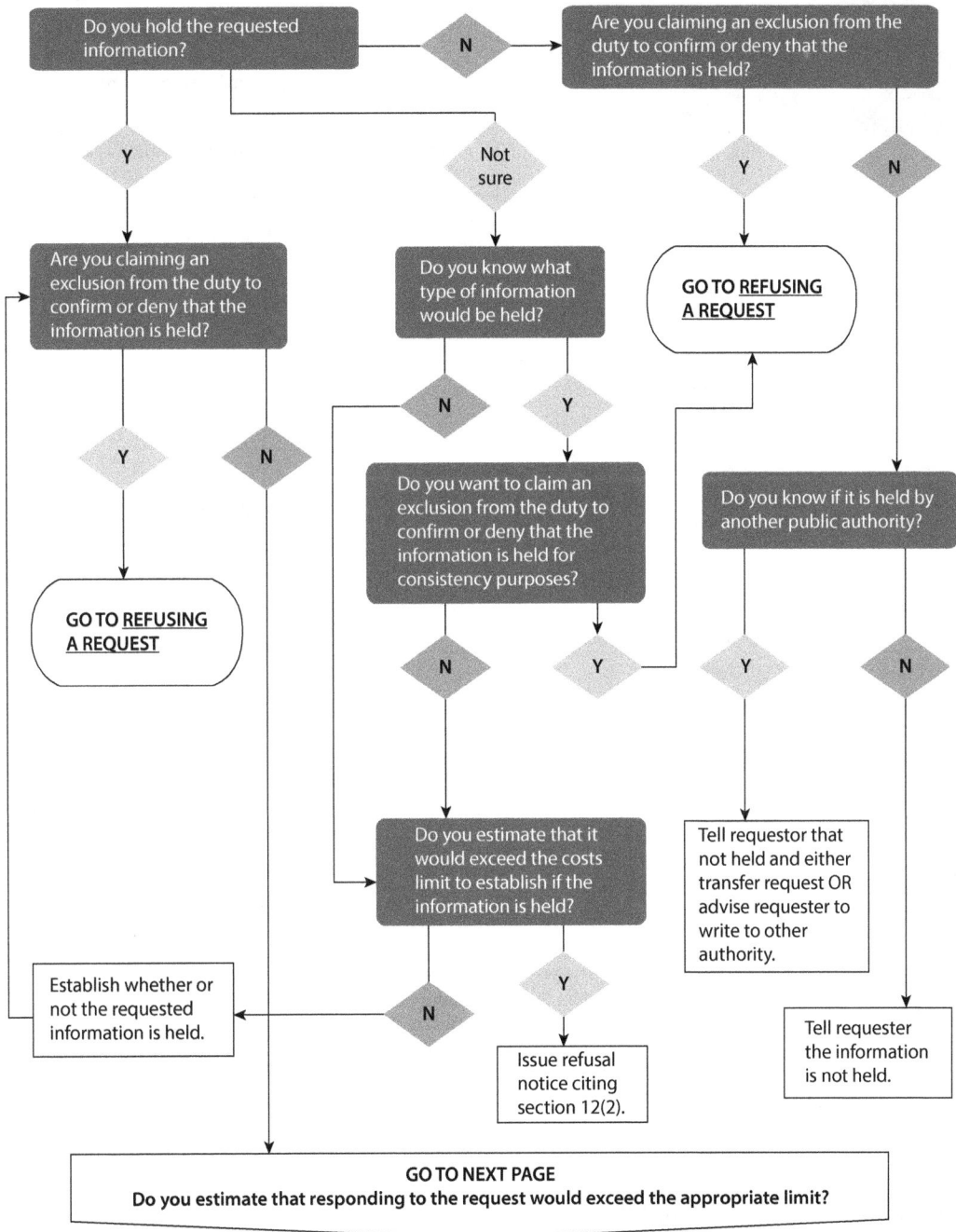

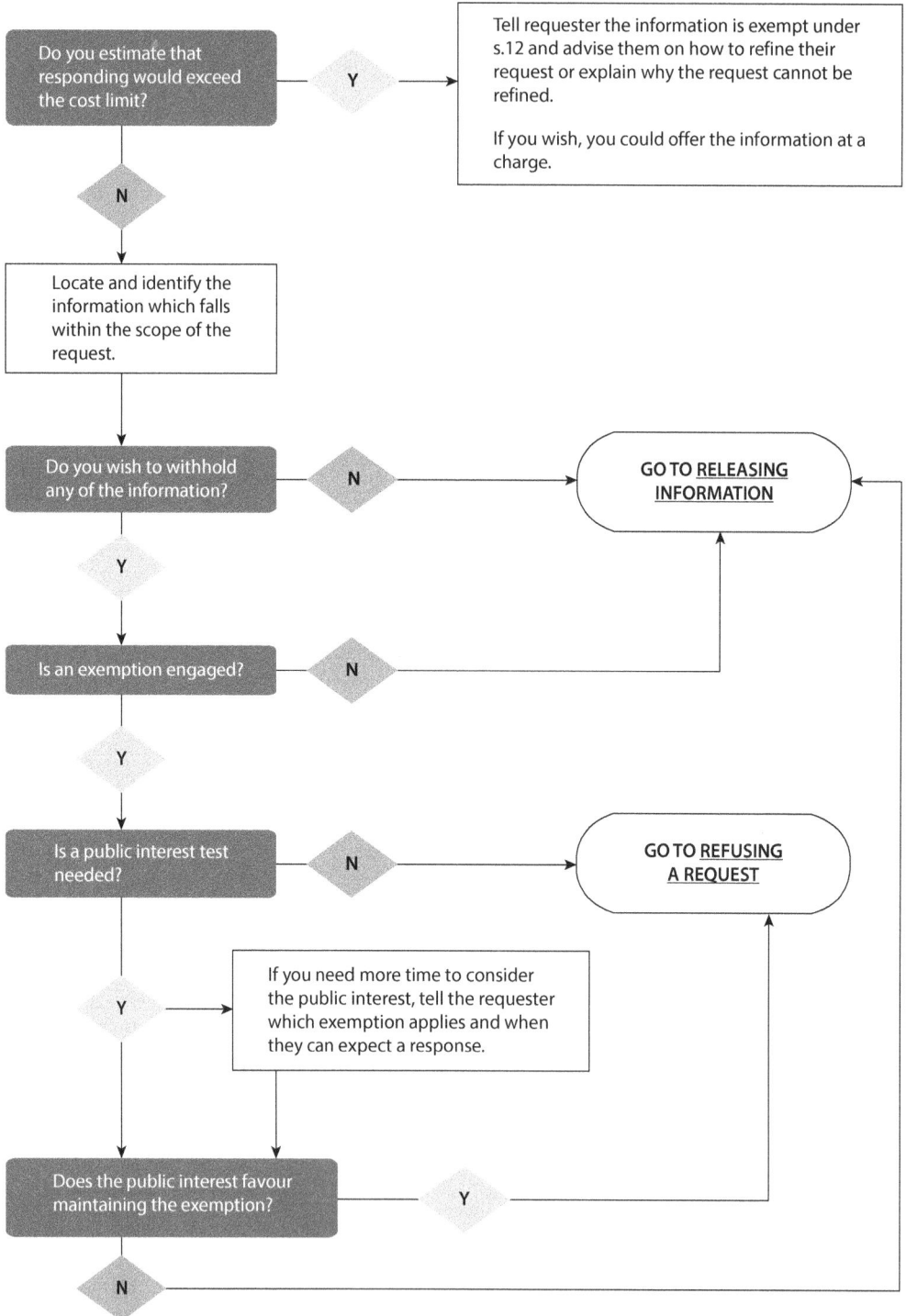

ico.
Information Commissioner's Office

RELEASING INFORMATION

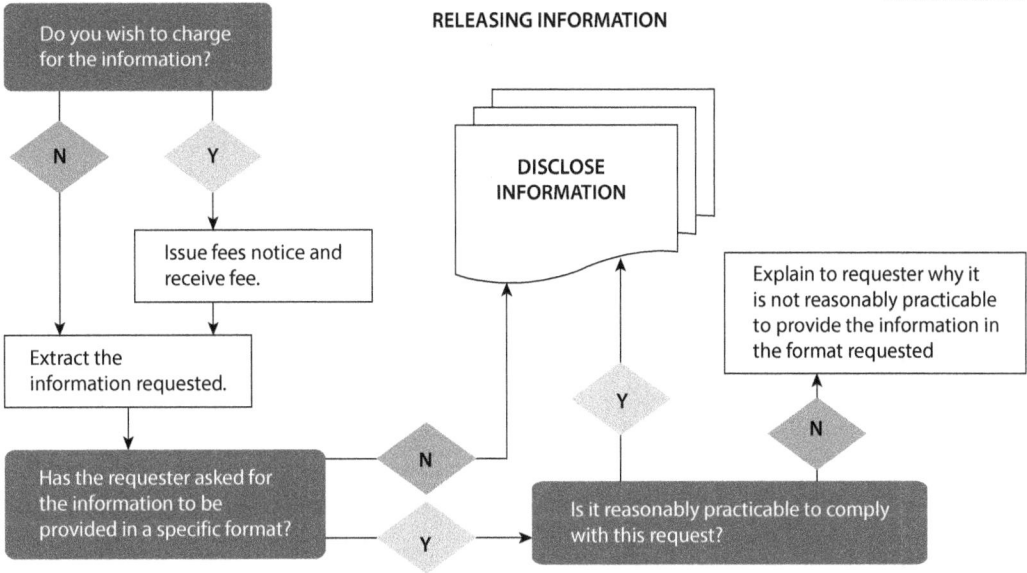

Do you wish to charge for the information?

N   Y

Issue fees notice and receive fee.

DISCLOSE INFORMATION

Explain to requester why it is not reasonably practicable to provide the information in the format requested

Extract the information requested.

Y

N

Has the requester asked for the information to be provided in a specific format?

N

Y

Is it reasonably practicable to comply with this request?

REFUSING A REQUEST

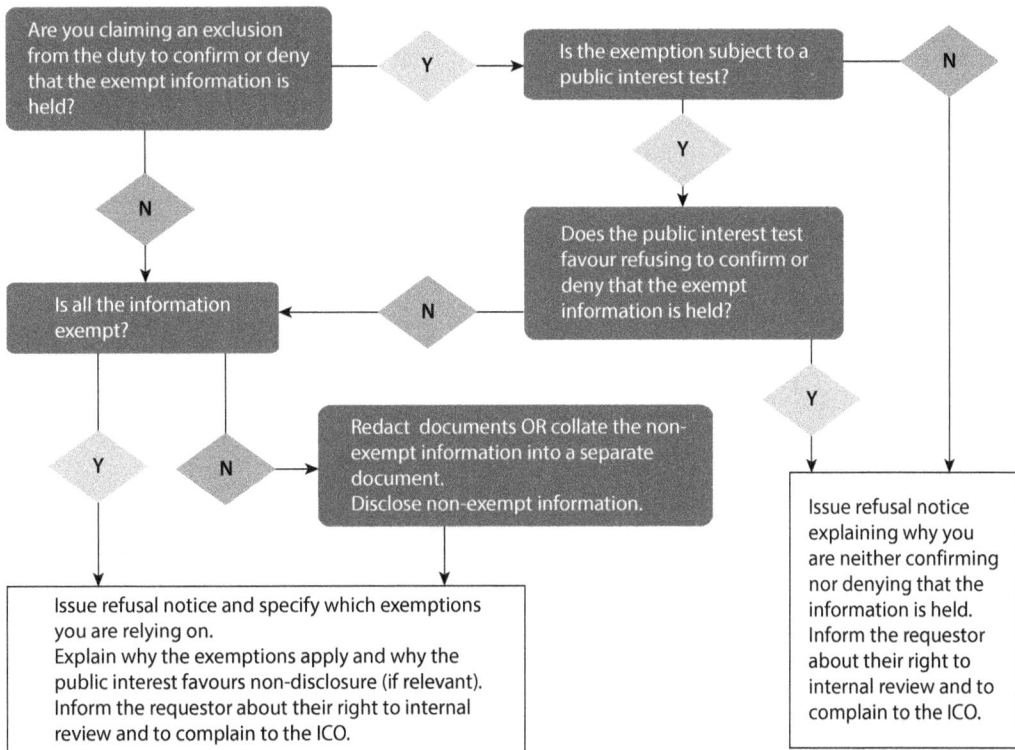

Are you claiming an exclusion from the duty to confirm or deny that the exempt information is held?

Y

Is the exemption subject to a public interest test?

N

N

Y

Is all the information exempt?

N

Does the public interest test favour refusing to confirm or deny that the exempt information is held?

Y   N

Y

Redact documents OR collate the non-exempt information into a separate document.
Disclose non-exempt information.

Issue refusal notice and specify which exemptions you are relying on.
Explain why the exemptions apply and why the public interest favours non-disclosure (if relevant).
Inform the requestor about their right to internal review and to complain to the ICO.

Issue refusal notice explaining why you are neither confirming nor denying that the information is held.
Inform the requestor about their right to internal review and to complain to the ICO.

Note: FOI/FOIA = Freedom of Information Act; IFO = Information Commissioner's Office.

Records Management and Risk-Related Standards

Generally Accepted Record-Keeping Principles

The principles provide a high-level overview of the principles of information governance. They were developed by ARMA International to foster awareness of information governance standards and principles and to assist organizations in developing information management systems with which records and information assets are expected to comply. The principles set forth the characteristics of an effective information governance program but allow flexibility based upon the unique circumstances of an organization's size, sophistication, legal environment, and resources.

Principle of Accountability
A senior executive (or a person of comparable authority) shall oversee the information governance program and delegate responsibility for records and information management to appropriate individuals. The organization adopts policies and procedures to guide personnel and ensure that the program can be audited.

Principle of Integrity
An information governance program shall be constructed so the information generated by or managed for the organization has a reasonable and suitable guarantee of authenticity and reliability.

Principle of Protection
An information governance program shall be constructed to ensure a reasonable level of protection for records and information that are private, confidential, privileged, secret, classified, or essential to business continuity or that otherwise require protection.

Principle of Compliance

An information governance program should be constructed to comply with applicable laws and other binding authorities, as well as with the organization's policies.

Principle of Availability

An organization shall maintain records and information in a manner that ensures timely, efficient, and accurate retrieval of needed information.

Principle of Retention

An organization shall maintain its records and information for an appropriate time, taking into account its legal, regulatory, fiscal, operational, and historical requirements.

Principle of Disposition

An organization shall provide secure and appropriate disposition for records and information that are no longer required to be maintained by applicable laws and the organization's policies.

Principle of Transparency

An organization's business processes and activities, including its information governance program, shall be documented in an open and verifiable manner, and that documentation shall be available to all personnel and appropriate interested parties.

Noark 4: Norwegian Record-Keeping System—Version 4

Noark 4 is a specification of functional requirements for electronic record-keeping systems used in public administration in Norway. The specification lists requirements with regard to information content (what kind of information it should be possible to register and retrieve), data structure (design of each data element and the relationship between these elements), and functionality (the functions that the systems are to maintain). In some cases there are requirements with regard to the user interface (how the systems communicate with the users), but this is mainly left to the individual system developers or vendors to decide. The specification does not contain requirements with regard to how the data structure is to be implemented or with regard to system design. This is left to the system developers.

Noark 5: Standard for Records Management

Noark 5 sets out requirements concerning record structure, metadata, and functionality but does not contain any requirements concerning how these requirements should actually be met in system development. Noark 5 therefore does not define a system but facilitates different solutions. The requirements are more strict for depositing, transfer, and migration. Obligatory metadata must be included in the export, and the export must have a defined structure. The standard does not contain a description of procedures or the way in which different requirements can be met.

ISO 14721: Space Data and Information Transfer Systems—Open Archival Information System (OAIS)—Reference Model

The standard establishes a common framework of terms and concepts that make up an open archival information system (OAIS). It allows existing and future archives to be meaningfully compared and contrasted. It provides a basis for further standardization within an archival context, and it should promote greater vendor awareness of, and support of, archival requirements. An OAIS is an archive that has accepted the responsibility to preserve information and make it available for a designated community. The information being maintained has been deemed to need long-term preservation, even if the OAIS itself is not permanent. "Long term" is long enough to be concerned with the impacts of changing technologies, including support for new media and data formats, or with a changing user community. Long term may extend indefinitely. In this reference model there is a particular focus on digital information, both as the primary forms of information held and as supporting information for both digitally and physically archived materials.

ISO 15489:2001: Records Management

ISO 15489 is the foundation standard which codifies best practice for records management operations.

ISO 15489, Part 1: *General* gives a high-level framework for record keeping and explains the benefits of good records management, the legal considerations, and the importance of making someone responsible for record keeping. This part also looks at what is needed for good records management, designing record-keeping systems, records management processes, auditing, and training.

ISO 15489, Part 2: *Guidelines* is a guide to putting the advice given in Part 1 into practice. It provides specific detail on developing records management policy and responsibility statements and suggests a process for developing record-keeping systems. It also provides advice about developing records processes and controls. It also gives specific advice about setting up monitoring, auditing, and training programs.

ISO 16175-1:2010: Information and Documentation—Principles and Functional Requirements for Records in Electronic Office Environments—Part 1: Overview and Statement of Principles

ISO 16175-1 establishes fundamental principles and functional requirements for software used to create and manage digital records in office environments. It is intended to be used in conjunction with ISO 16175-2 and ISO 16175-3. ISO 16175-1 establishes the principles of good practice, guiding principles, and implementation guidelines, and it lists risks and mitigations for purposes including enabling better management of records in organizations, supporting the business needs of an organization by enabling greater effectiveness and efficiency of the operations, providing enhanced abilities to support auditing activities, improving capabilities to comply with statutory mandates specified in various information-related legislation (for example, data protection and privacy), supporting good governance (for example, accountability, transparency, and enhanced service delivery) through good management of records, and maximizing cross-jurisdictional consistency regarding the articulation of functional requirements for managing records.

ISO 16175-2:2011: Information and Documentation—Principles and Functional Requirements for Records in Electronic Office Environments—Part 2: Guidelines and Functional Requirements for Digital Records Management Systems

ISO 16175-2 articulates a set of functional requirements for digital records management systems. These requirements apply to records irrespective of the media in which they were created and/or stored. It is applicable to products that are often termed "electronic records management systems" or "enterprise content management systems." ISO 16175-2 uses the term "digital records management systems" for those software applications whose primary function is records management. It does not seek to set requirements for records still in use and held within business systems. Digital objects created by e-mail, word processing, spreadsheet, and imaging applications (such as text documents and still or moving images), where they are identified to be of business value, are managed within digital records management systems that meet the functional requirements established in ISO 16175-2.

Records managed by a digital records management system can be stored on a variety of different media formats and can be managed in hybrid record aggregations that include both digital and nondigital elements. ISO 16175-2 does not give specifications for the long-term preservation of digital records; this issue needs to be addressed separately within a dedicated framework for digital preservation or "digital archiving" at the strategic level. These digital preservation considerations transcend the life of systems and are system independent; they need to be assessed in a specific migration and conversion plan at the tactical level. However, recognition of the need to maintain records for as long as they are required is addressed in ISO 16175-2, and potential format obsolescence issues need to be considered when applying the functional requirements.

ISO 16175-3:2010: Information and Documentation—Principles and Functional Requirements for Records in Electronic Office Environments—Part 3: Guidelines and Functional Requirements for Records in Business Systems

ISO 16175-3 specifies general requirements and guidelines for records management and gives guidelines for the appropriate identification and management of evidence (records) of business activities transacted through business systems. It provides guidelines to assist in understanding processes and requirements for identifying and managing records in business systems; developing requirements for functionality for records to be included in a design specification when building, upgrading, or purchasing business system software; evaluating the records management capability of proposed customized or commercial off-the-shelf business system software; and reviewing the functionality for records or assess compliance of existing business systems.

ISO 16175-3 specifies requirements for export supports preservation by allowing the export of records to a system that is capable of long-term preservation activities or for the ongoing migration of records into new systems. It does not specify requirements for the long-term preservation of digital records, and it is not applicable to records management in highly integrated software environments based on service-oriented architectures.

ISO 16363:2012: Space Data and Information Transfer Systems—Audit and Certification of Trustworthy Digital Repositories

This standard is for use as the basis for providing audit and certification of the trustworthiness of digital repositories. It provides a detailed specification of criteria by which digital repositories shall be audited. This document is meant primarily for those responsible for auditing digital repositories and for those who work in or are responsible for digital repositories seeking objective measurement of the trustworthiness of their repository. Some institutions may also choose to use these metrics during a design or redesign process for their digital repository.

ISO 23081: Information and Documentation—Records Management Processes—Metadata for Records

Part 1: Principles
ISO 23081 sets a framework for creating, managing, and using records management metadata and explains the principles that govern them. It is a guide to understanding, implementing, and using metadata within the framework of ISO 15489. It addresses the relevance of records management metadata in business processes and the different roles and types of metadata that support business and records management processes. It also sets a framework for managing those metadata. It assesses the main existing metadata sets in line with the requirements of ISO 15489.

Part 2: Conceptual and Implementation Issues

This part of ISO 23081 focuses on the framework for defining metadata elements for managing records and provides a generic statement of metadata elements, whether these are physical, analogue, or digital, consistent with the principles of ISO 23081-1.

ISO 26122: Information and Documentation—Work Process Analysis for Records

This standard provides guidance on work process analysis from the perspective of the creation, capture, and control of records. It identifies two types of analyses, namely, functional analysis (decomposition of functions into processes) and sequential analysis (investigation of the flow of transactions). Each analysis entails a preliminary review of context (i.e., mandate and regulatory environment) appropriate for the analysis. The components of the analysis can be undertaken in various combinations and in a different order from that described here, depending on the nature of the task, the scale of the project, and the purpose of the analysis. Guidance provided in the form of lists of questions/matters to be considered under each element of the analysis is also included.

The standard describes a practical application of the theory outlined in ISO 15489. As such, it is independent of technology (i.e., it can be applied regardless of the technological environment), although it can be used to assess the adequacy of technical tools that support an organization's work processes.

ISO/IEC 27001:2013: Information Technology—Security Techniques— Information Security Management Systems—Requirements

This standard specifies the requirements for establishing, implementing, maintaining, and continually improving an information security management system within the context of the organization. This standard also includes requirements for the assessment and treatment of information security risks tailored to the needs of the organization.

The standard covers information security leadership and high-level support for policy, planning an information security management system, risk assessment, risk treatment, supporting an information security management system, making an information security management system operational, reviewing the system's performance, and corrective action.

ISO 30300:2011: Information and Documentation—Management Systems for Records—Fundamentals and Vocabulary

This standard defines terms and definitions applicable to the standards on a management system for records (MSR) prepared by ISO/TC 46/SC 11. It also establishes the objectives for using an MSR, provides principles for an MSR, describes a process approach, and specifies roles for top management. It is applicable to any type of organization that wishes to establish, implement, maintain, and improve an MSR to support its business, ensure itself of conformity with its stated records policy, and demonstrate conformity with this standard by undertaking a self-assessment and self-declaration. It also supports organizations seeking confirmation of its self-declaration by a party external to the organization or seeking certification of its MSR by an external party.

ISO 31000:2012: Risk Management—Principles and Guidelines

The standard provides principles, a framework, and a process for managing risk. It can be used by any organization regardless of its size, activity, or sector. Using ISO 31000 can help organizations increase the likelihood of achieving objectives, improve the identification of opportunities and threats, and effectively allocate and use resources for risk treatment. However, ISO 31000 cannot be used for certification purposes but does provide guidance for internal or external audit programs. Organizations using it can compare their risk management practices with an internationally recognized benchmark, providing sound principles for effective management and corporate governance.

An Overview of Exemptions in Nine Countries

Table F.1 An Overview of Exemptions in Nine Countries

Country	Exemption provisions in RTI laws
Albania	*FOI (2010) 17: Exemptions to disclosure requirements*
	FOI (2010) 18: Exemptions to coverage:
	Article 17 of the constitution (1998), which provides for limitations on rights, but only in accordance with the standards articulated in the ECHR
	Article 4 of the Law on the Right to Information (1999)
	Article 1 of the Law on Information classified "State Secret" (1999)
	Articles 19 and 54 of the Code of Administrative Procedure (1999)
	Articles 1 and 2 of Law on Protection of Personal Data (2008)
	Articles 56, 62, 63, 65, 69 of the Law on Archives (2003)
	Specifically, Article 19 of the Code of Administrative Procedure (1999) and Article 63 of the Law on Archives (2003) exempt state secrets and personal data from disclosure
	According to Article 65 of the Law on Archives (2003), access to a host of other categories may be partly restricted as well. These categories include information pertaining to the following: foreign relations, public security, criminal investigations, commerce and economic competition, fiscal and monetary policy, sensitive environmental information, governmental inspections and controls, the "equality of the parties in conflicts," good-faith administrative decision making, and individuals' legal interests.
	Exemption can be overridden
	FOI (2010) 19: Public interest test:
	Article 66 of the Law on Archives (2003) provides the accessibility of archival records if a higher public interest legitimates that access
	FOI (2010) 21: Harm test:
	Article 5 of the Law on Information classified "State Secret" (1999) provides that the information cannot be classified as a state or an official secret if doing so will have a negative impact on the implementation of specific state and branch development programs.
	Article 10 of the Law on Information classified "State Secret" (1999) provides information on cases that are prohibited to be classified.

table continues next page

Table F.1 An Overview of Exemptions in Nine Countries *(continued)*

Country	Exemption provisions in RTI laws
India	*FOI (2010) 17: Exemptions to disclosure requirements* *FOI (2010) 18: Exemptions to coverage:* Section 8 of the Right to Information Act (2005) provides exemptions from disclosure of information or grounds on which furnishing of information by a public authority may be refused. The grounds identified under Section 8 for such refusal broadly relate to public policy, interests of the state, or protection of established principles of law. The exemptions cover areas of national security, law enforcement intelligence gathering, commercial interests, privacy, parliamentary privileges, Cabinet papers, and foreign relations. Subsection (2) and (3) to Section 8 contemplate carve-outs from the above mentioned exceptions, that is, they permit disclosure of information where public good by disclosure outweighs the harm to protected interests and where the requested information relates to an event, occurrence, or matter that is 20 years old or more (sunset clause). The sunset clause applies only to seven out of 10 categories listed in Section 8. Section 9 protects information that, if furnished, would amount to copyright infringement subsisting in a person other than the state. Schedule II to the Right to Information Act (2005) lists 22 security- and intelligence-related organizations that are partially excluded from the coverage of the law. More organizations and divisions and sections of departments are excluded under this section by the state governments within their jurisdiction. The organizations excluded under Schedule II must provide information relating to allegations of corruption and human rights violations. Information regarding allegations of human rights violations will be given with the approval of the concerned Information Commission. Exemptions are of internationally recognized security, integrity, strategic, scientific, and economic concerns. Also exempt is information that can endanger the life or safety of persons or reveal identity of confidential informers, as well as information that could impede the investigation, apprehension, or prosecution of offenders. Fiduciary information is also exempt. Cabinet papers are exempt only till the decision is taken. Section 8(1) also states "Provided that the information which cannot be denied to the Parliament or a State Legislature shall not be denied to any person." *Exemption can be overridden* *FOI (2010) 19: Public Interest test:* Section 8 of the Right to Information Act (2005) provides for certain qualified exemptions, which are subject to the public interest test. Here the public authority in possession of the information must consider whether there is greater public interest in disclosing the information or withholding the information (popularly called balancing the public interest or herein referred to as the public interest test). Public interest in such circumstances would hold the key while making the decision whether the information is to be withheld or disclosed. Public interest, in the opinion of the Supreme Court of India, has been expressed by way of Supreme Court guidelines for maintaining a Public Interest Litigation, 1998, and in cases such as *Janta Dal v. VHS Choudhary, S P Gupta v. President of India*, or *State of Gujarat v. Mirzapur Moti Kureshi Kasab Jamat* and others. Section 22 of the Right to Information Act (2005) specifies that in the case of inconsistency with any other act, including the Official Secrets Act, the RTI Act will prevail. *FOI (2010) 21: Harm test:* According to Section 8(2) of the Right to Information Act (2005), even where there is harm, if the public interest is greater, the information must be disclosed.

table continues next page

Table F.1 An Overview of Exemptions in Nine Countries *(continued)*

Country	Exemption provisions in RTI laws
Jordan	*FOI (2010) 17: Exemptions to disclosure requirements* *FOI (2010) 18: Exemptions to coverage:* Specific exemptions to coverage are outlined in Articles 10 and 13 of the Law on Guarantee of Access to Information (2007). They include state secrets, other secret documents, correspondence between government agencies, individual personal files, personal correspondence with government agencies, information that if revealed may affect negotiations with other countries, investigation materials, and commercial, industrial, and financial or economic information that, if revealed, may cause harm. Articles 3, 6, 8, and 10 of the Law on the Protection of State Secrets and Documents (1971) contain exemptions related to national security, military operations, international relations, intelligence, arms, and ammunition. *Exemption can be overridden* *FOI (2010) 19: Public interest test:* No relevant legal provision *FOI (2010) 21: Harm test:* No relevant legal provision
Mexico	*FOI (2010) 17: Exemptions to disclosure requirements* *FOI (2010) 18: Exemptions to coverage:* Articles 13 and 14 of the Law on Transparency and Access to Public Information (2002) list the reasons for classifying information as reserved. Such reasons include information that might harm national security, public security, national defense, foreign relations, the economy or currency, individuals' health or safety, law enforcement or prosecution, tax collections, immigration enforcement, commercial or banking secrets, trade secrets, investigations, court records, and public servant accountability procedures. Preliminary deliberative processes, opinions, and communications are also exempt. The classification is made by the highest responsible officer in every unit according to the law, regulations, and other applicable guidelines (Article 16). The files are reserved in their custody (Article 17). Confidential information is the personal information given by individuals to the obligated subjects (Article 18). To disclose such information, the consent of the person concerned is required (Article 19), except in those cases of Article 22 or in the cases where the information lies on public registries and public sources (Article 18). Article 13 of Recommendations for Identifying Reserved or Confidential information (2003) outlines the exceptions to the confidential information. *Exemption can be overridden* *FOI (2010) 19: Public interest test:* No relevant legal provision *FOI (2010) 21: Harm test:* No relevant legal provision
Moldova	*FOI (2010) 17: Exemptions to disclosure requirements* *FOI (2010) 18: Exemptions to coverage:* Article 7 of Law on Access to Information (2000) (along with Article 1 of the Law on State Secrets [2008]) provides the limits of the right to access information and lists the criteria to be adopted to apply such restrictions (i.e., the requested information involves another individual's rights and reputation, national security and public order, public health and morals) and the types of information that are exempted from coverage (i.e., state secrets implicating defense, economy, science and techniques, foreign relations, state security, enforcement of public order and activities of public authorities, intelligence, and state security; commercial secrets; personal data; and sensitive information about investigations and scientific research).

table continues next page

Table F.1 An Overview of Exemptions in Nine Countries *(continued)*

Country	Exemption provisions in RTI laws
	Exemptions to coverage are further defined in the corresponding laws, such as the Law on State Secrets (2008) and the Law on Protection of Personal Data (1994).
	Exemption can be overridden
	FOI (2010) 19: Public interest test:
	Article 1(2) of the Law on State Secrets (2008) stipulates that it is prohibited to restrict any information that limits the access to information of public interest
	FOI (2010) 21: Harm test:
	Article 1(2) of the Law on State Secrets (2008) stipulates that it is prohibited to restrict any information whose nondisclosure negatively impacts the state and branch development programs or discourages the competition among economic agents.
	Article 7(5) of Law on Access to Information (2000) provides for harm/prejudice test in the case of information with limited access. As such, the provision stipulates that no restriction shall be imposed when the disclosure of classified information will not cause any harm to national security or when the benefit of such disclosure was greater than the prejudice caused by it.
Romania	*FOI (2010) 17: Exemptions to disclosure requirements*
	FOI (2010) 18: Exemptions to coverage:
	Article 12 of the Law on Freedom of Information (2001) provides for exemptions from free access to information, including that which implicates national security and public order, the country's economic and political interests, commercial or financial activities that might prejudice fair competition, personal data, ongoing investigations and judicial procedures, and the protection of youth. These and other exemptions from the FOI regime are regulated by the following laws: Article 13 of the Law on Freedom of Information (2001); Article 9(2) of the Law on the Functioning and Organization of the External Information Service (1998); Article 10(2) of the Law on the Functioning and Organization of the External Information Service (1998); Article 16 of the Law on Classified Information (2002); Articles 17 and 31 of the Law on Classified Information (2002); Article 12 of the Law on National Security (1991); and Article 5 of the Law on Transparency in the Decision Making Process (2003).
	These latter provisions provide that certain information pertaining to the following subjects is exempt from disclosure: national security, national defense, the military, topographic maps and geological information, national energy sources, technology or science, the economy or the nation's currency, personal data, and foreign relations
	Exemption can be overridden
	FOI (2010) 19: Public interest test:
	Articles 13 of the Law on Freedom of Information (2001) provides that information implicating officials' illegal acts cannot be classified. Instead, such information is "of public interest."
	Article 33 of the Law on Classified Information (2002) provides other circumstances when classification is prohibited. Article 33 prohibits classification of information as commercial secrets if the public interest is strong enough, or if the information implicates illegal activity, or if such classification may be qualified as obstructing justice.
	Article 5 of the Law on Personal Data (2001) provides for circumstances when personal data may be disclosed with the consent of the person and for the circumstances when such consent is overridden by the greater interests of justice. Such interests include the fair execution of contracts, public interest, health, life, and physical integrity of a person, among others.

table continues next page

Table F.1 An Overview of Exemptions in Nine Countries *(continued)*

Country	Exemption provisions in RTI laws
	FOI (2010) 21: Harm test:
	Article 14 of the Law on Freedom of Information (2001) provides that information implicating citizens' personal data may be considered "of public interest"—and therefore may not be classified—to the extent that it affects the capacity to exercise a public function. Put another way, if to the extent that it harms the capacity to carry out public functions, personal data may be disclosed.
Uganda	*FOI (2010) 17: Exemptions to disclosure requirements*
	FOI (2010) 18: Exemptions to coverage:
	According to Article 41(1) of the constitution (1995), information that may be prejudicial to national security or may interfere with state sovereignty or the right to individual privacy may not be disclosed. The classification of such information is not specified in the constitution, but Subsection 2 of Article 41 of the constitution states that parliament shall make laws classifying information and procedure for obtaining access to the information referred to in Subsection 1.
	According to Articles 25 through 34 of the Access to Information Act (2005), access to certain information may be denied. Information exempt from coverage includes cabinet minutes; privacy of persons; commercial information of third parties; certain confidential information; safety of persons and property; law enforcement and legal proceedings; privileged legal records; records pertaining to defense, security, and international relations; and records regarding the operation of public bodies.
	Exemption can be overridden
	FOI (2010) 19: Public interest test:
	Article 34 of the Access to Information Act (2005) provides exceptions to certain information exempt from coverage based on the public interest test.
	FOI (2010) 21: Harm test:
	Articles 26 (3), 27 (2), 28 (2), 31 (2), 32 (2), and 33 (2) of the Access to Information Act (2005) provide for exceptions to certain exempt information that could be disclosed and would not prejudice or endanger the subject of the exemption being claimed.
United Kingdom	*FOI (2010) 17: Exemptions to disclosure requirements*
	FOI (2010) 18: Exemptions to coverage:
	According to the Freedom of Information Act (2000), Part II, Sections 21–44, there are 23 exemptions, including information implicating the following:
	National security, intelligence, communications, the military, certain tribunals, national defense, foreign and intra-U.K. relations or international correspondences, the national economy, parliamentary privileges, criminal investigations, legal proceedings, the proper administration of justice, preliminary work on government policy, ministerial or royal communications or the operation of ministers' private offices, the frank provision of advice or effective discharge of certain offices' responsibilities, individuals' health and safety, sensitive environmental information, personal data, legal professional privilege, trade secrets, and anyone's commercial interests.
	Also, information may be exempt if it was obtained by a third party in confidence, or on the basis of either "absolute" or "qualified" protections.
	According to Section 30(3) of the Data Protection Act (1998), the Secretary of State may, with certain limitations, exempt government-processed personal information from the Act's disclosure requirements.

table continues next page

Table F.1 An Overview of Exemptions in Nine Countries *(continued)*

Country	Exemption provisions in RTI laws
	Exemption can be overridden
	FOI (2010) 19: Public interest test:
	Part I, Section 2, of the Freedom of Information Act (2000) applies a public interest test to 17 of the act's 23 exemption provisions.
	The public interest is not defined. Section 2 merely provides that information can be withheld if the public interest in upholding the relevant exemption outweighs the public interest in disclosure.
	FOI (2010) 21: Harm test:
	According to Section 30(3) of the Data Protection Act (1998), the Secretary of State may not exempt government information unless disclosing the requested personal information would "be likely to prejudice the carrying out of social work."
United States	*FOI (2010) 17: Exemptions to disclosure requirements*
	FOI (2010) 18: Exemptions to coverage:
	According to Section (b) of the FOIA (1966), an agency may refuse to disclose an agency record (or portion thereof) that falls within any of the FOIA's nine statutory exemptions. The exemptions protect against the disclosure of information that would harm national defense or foreign policy, privacy of individuals, proprietary interests of business, functioning of the government, law enforcement, and other important interests, or that contains geological data.
	The Intelligence Authorization Act (2002) amends FOIA by asserting that intelligence agencies need not disclose information to any government entity (or any representative thereof) requesting information unless it is a U.S. government entity.
	Exemption can be overridden
	FOI (2010) 19: Public interest test:
	No relevant legal provision
	FOI (2010) 21: Harm test:
	Under the FOIA (1966), all exemptions except for part of Exemption 2 and arguably a part of Exemption 7(E) involve determinations of how harmful disclosure would be. As a matter of policy in the Obama administration (just as it was in the Clinton administration), agencies must apply a "foreseeable harm" standard for defending agency decisions to withhold information. Under this standard, the Department of Justice will defend an agency's denial of a FOIA request "only if (1) the agency reasonably foresees that disclosure would harm an interest protected by one of the statutory exemptions, or (2) disclosure is prohibited by law." Agencies must also include the "foreseeable harm" standard as part of the FOIA analysis at the initial request stage and at the administrative appeal stage.
	Also, FOIA (1966) Sections (b)6 and (b)7(C) assert that certain exemptions to disclosure do not apply if they reasonably constitute an unwarranted invasion of privacy.

Source: World Bank 2015, "Public Accountability Mechanisms," https://agidata.org/pam/ProfileListByAbc.aspx.
Note: ECHR = European Convention on Human Rights; FOI/FOIA = Freedom of Information Act; RTI = right to information.

Environmental Benefits Statement

The World Bank Group is committed to reducing its environmental footprint. In support of this commitment, the Publishing and Knowledge Division leverages electronic publishing options and print-on-demand technology, which is located in regional hubs worldwide. Together, these initiatives enable print runs to be lowered and shipping distances decreased, resulting in reduced paper consumption, chemical use, greenhouse gas emissions, and waste.

The Publishing and Knowledge Division follows the recommended standards for paper use set by the Green Press Initiative. The majority of our books are printed on Forest Stewardship Council (FSC)–certified paper, with nearly all containing 50–100 percent recycled content. The recycled fiber in our book paper is either unbleached or bleached using totally chlorine-free (TCF), processed chlorine-free (PCF), or enhanced elemental chlorine-free (EECF) processes.

More information about the Bank's environmental philosophy can be found at http://www.worldbank.org/corporateresponsibility.

green
press
INITIATIVE

www.ingramcontent.com/pod-product-compliance
Lightning Source LLC
Chambersburg PA
CBHW080424270326
41929CB00018B/3160